THE
JEWISH
DIETARY
LAWS

THE JEWISH DIETARY LAWS

Revised and Expanded Edition

THEIR MEANING FOR OUR TIME
Samuel H. Dresner

A GUIDE TO OBSERVANCE
Seymour Siegel

David M. Pollock

The Rabbinical Assembly

United Synagogue
Commission on Jewish Education

This expanded and revised volume has been prepared under the auspices of the Rabbinical Assembly of America and the Publications Committee of the United Synagogue Commission on Jewish Education.

INTRODUCTION

Rabbi Eleazar said: When the Israelites gave precedence to *"we will do"* over *"we will hearken,"* a Heavenly Voice went forth and exclaimed to them, "Who revealed to My children this secret . . .?"

What was that secret? It was that conduct affects belief. The way we live influences the way we think. In a word: we are what we do.

It has been more than two and a half decades since *The Jewish Dietary Laws*, by Rabbis Samuel Dresner and Seymour Siegel, was published. And it would seem that within that time span, increasing numbers of Jews have discovered that "secret." We think that the availability of this lucid booklet has helped immeasurably with that discovery.

What is Kashrut? What does its observance mean? What values are embodied in its rule and regulations? What are those rules and regulations? The answers to these questions are found in this comprehensive, useful and authoritative presentation.

RABBI JOEL H. ZAIMAN, *Chairman*
United Synagogue Commission on Jewish Education

CONTENTS

THE JEWISH DIETARY LAWS:

Their Meaning for Our Time

by SAMUEL H. DRESNER

Preface

There is a well-known story about a rabbi who, upon coming to a new congregation, was taken aside by the president and in a friendly manner advised not to talk about certain topics from the pulpit: Hebrew Schools —because the children had to take music and dancing lessons and needed the afternoons for play; the Sabbath—because in America one was compelled to work on the Sabbath to make a living, and making a living came first; the Dietary Laws, Kashrut—because it was only an ancient health measure, out of place in modern times and, furthermore, too much trouble for the women to bother with two sets of dishes. The rabbi, surprised at the counsel he was receiving, asked anxiously: "If I cannot talk about Hebrew Schools and I cannot talk about the Sabbath and I cannot talk about Kashrut, what can I talk about?" The president replied in mild astonishment: "Why, that is no problem at all, Rabbi; *just talk about Judaism!*"

This story, bitter though it may sound, reflects a good deal of what has passed for Jewish life in the past decades in America. I say in the past decades, because matters have been changing considerably of late. And to the better. The concrete nature of Judaism is being more and more realized. We are coming to understand in an ever deeper fashion that our faith cannot be reduced so easily to a list of abstractions, that Judaism means Hebrew Schools, Sabbath and Kashrut. Jewish education, for example, has in the last ten years become a major concern of the American Jewish community. Tremendous efforts and vast amounts of money are at present being expended to raise educational standards, to increase student enrollment, intensify curricula and provide for better qualified teachers. The Sabbath, too, has undergone a national "revitalization" campaign through the auspices of one of the major Jewish movements in America. Books and articles have been published, classes in the observance of the Sabbath have been arranged and thousands of sermons devoted solely to this subject. But, while Hebrew education and, to a lesser degree but still noticeably, Sabbath observance have been brought to the attention of the American Jewish community, as yet, Kashrut has been consistently overlooked. The voice of that Synagogue president still dins in the ears of most of our leaders, and where the matter of Kashrut is concerned, they are mute. Rarely is an article written on the subject, rarely a sermon preached on the topic. It is ignored, passed over in silence, as if it did not exist, as if there were no crisis in Kashrut.

Of course, good reasons may be presented for this neglect. The movement away from Kashrut has been tremendous. No one will question the fact that there are far fewer Kosher homes in today's generation than in the past generation. Jewish leaders have been so busy attempting to achieve the simple task of Synagogue affiliation and some regularity in Synagogue attendance that a subject such as Kashrut, with all the difficulties and hardships it presents—apart from the lack of a satisfying modern formulation of its meaning and relevance—was virtually anathema. From a purely pedagogic point of view, then, it seemed wiser to devote the limited energies at hand to those aspects of Jewish life which promised easier and better results. And there is much to be said for this argument. Yet, we might well ask ourselves—even from the point of view of pedagogy—whether the time is not ripe for a facing up to this problem. There has been a return to the Synagogue on the part of our people. There is a mild renaissance of interest in things Jewish, especially in the area of religious values.[1] The real problem today is no longer one of membership. That has, to some extent, been achieved. It is rather a matter of deepening the religious consciousness of that membership, making it aware of Jewish teaching, bringing it to Jewish commitment, leading it back to the path of Jewish observance. American Jews have been told that they must belong to a Synagogue, but they have not as yet been told *what belonging to a Synagogue means.* Furthermore, if we look at the subject somewhat more closely, we can find scattered here and there small but significant numbers—growing numbers—of younger men and women who, discovering Judaism for themselves as something new and vital, and free from the prejudices which hampered their parents, have eagerly accepted Kashrut into their personal life, primarily as a means of identifying themselves with their people. The response to an intelligently conducted campaign, a call to Kashrut, sounded in our communities and congregations, may be more positive than we think. There is a spark in every Jewish heart which needs only to be kindled with insight and meaning. It is the purpose of this essay to contribute toward a modern rationale for Kashrut which will contain both of these elements.

I believe that the reasons for the diminished observance of Kashrut in our time are twofold: First, the lack of *knowledge about it*, and, secondly, the lack of the *will to do it*. Let us analyze the problem in that order.

I

THE PROBLEM OF UNDERSTANDING

Not Health but Holiness

Knowledge about Kashrut is, at best, minimal. It is more misunderstood than understood. The most common misconception regarding Kashrut is that it is an ancient health measure which may have had its place in antiquity but, what with modern methods of slaughtering, regular government inspection and sanitary food preparation, is quite clearly an anachronism which should be discarded along with the horse and carriage and the high-button shoe. But is health really the purpose of Kashrut? Of course, one must not overlook the concern for disease and the attempt to achieve purity in the Kosher laws; still we must ask the question again: is health the *primary* concern of Kashrut? Let us turn to the Biblical text for an answer.

In Leviticus (11:44-45), after we are told which animals, fowl and fish are permitted and which forbidden, the reason for this long series of laws is at last given: "I am the Lord your God; sanctify yourselves therefore, and be *holy*; for I am holy. . . . For I am the Lord that brought you up out of the land of Egypt to be your God; ye shall therefore be *holy*." In Deuteronomy (14:21) we read: "Ye shall not eat anything that dieth of itself . . .; for thou art a *holy* people unto the Lord thy God. Thou shalt not seethe a kid in its mother's milk." In Exodus (22:30): "And ye shall be *holy* men unto Me; therefore ye shall not eat any flesh that is torn of the beasts of the field: ye shall cast it to the dogs." Each of these passages deals with a different aspect of Kashrut and yet in all of them the same word is repeated again and again: *Kadosh*, holy. This, then, is clearly the purpose and the goal of the Kosher laws: not *health* but *holiness*.

To Be Holy Means To Hallow

What does holiness mean in Judaism?

There are three great spiritual forces in the world which can be distinguished in terms of their attitude toward such basic drives of man as hunger, sex and the will to power: Paganism, Classical Christianity and Judaism. Let us compare them in their broadest outlines.

Paganism glorifies these elemental powers as such.

Christianity subjugates them.

Judaism hallows them.

Paganism worships the forces of nature.
Christianity denies them as sinful.
Judaism serves God by means of them.

Paganism says nature is holy and thereby unleashes
the beast within man.
Christianity says nature is unholy and thereby frus-
trates the natural desires of men.
Judaism says nature is neither holy nor unholy, but
is *waiting to be made holy* and thereby sublimates
the natural desires of man through a system of
mitzvot, to the service of God.

It is well to begin this discussion by contrasting
Judaism with these two other major spiritual forces,
because, though formulated somewhat differently and
called by a variety of names, the pagan and classical
Christian points of view have dominated the thinking
of mankind down through the centuries, including the
twentieth. Strangely enough, though opposites, the
Christian point of view, by virtue of its very misunder-
standing of human nature, has often led back to the
pagan view against which it first revolted. Thus the
shocking ancient pagan glorification of sex as holy and
the perversions which resulted from this view brought
about the later Christian degradation of sex as sinful,
which in turn produced and still produces a constant
renewal of the pagan view. Sigmund Freud has written
at length about this causal relationship.

"Power" may serve as another example. History
knows both the glorification of the will to power in the
cruel tyrant or the greedy unprincipled citizen as well

as the rejection of this world (and therefore any manner of "power") for the monastery and the world to come as typified by the Christian saint or the holy men of the Eastern religions who train themselves to no longer feel pleasure or pain or desire and reject the actual society of men for an entirely spiritual existence called Nirvana. In the first case power is used to an evil end. In the second case—often a reaction to the first—power is rejected as being evil in itself, and society remains as it was.

The teaching of Judaism is categorically different. It maintains that our world is neither to be deified nor vilified, glorified nor subjugated, worshiped nor despised. It is to be hallowed. And herein lies the hope of mankind.

Martin Buber has expressed this unique approach of Judaism in a succinct fashion:

"Judaism teaches us to overcome the fundamental separation between the holy and the profane. This separation has formed a part of the foundation of every religion. Everywhere the holy is removed and set apart from the fullness of things, properties and actions which belong to the universal, so that the holy becomes a self-contained holiness outside of which the profane must pitch its tent. The consequence of this separation in the history of man is a twofold one. Religion is thereby assured a firm province whose untouchableness is always guaranteed . . . but the holy is not given a corresponding power in the rest of life . . .

"In Judaism . . . one need only note how many everyday actions are introduced by a blessing to recognize how deep the hallowing reaches into what is in

itself unhallowed. One not only blesses God every
morning on awakening because he has allowed one to
awaken, but also when one begins to use a new house
or piece of clothing or tool because one has been preserved in life to this hour. Thus the simple fact of con-
tinued earthly existence is sanctified at each occasion
that offers itself and therefore this occasion itself also
. . . The separation between the realms is only a provi-
sional one . . . In the Messianic world all shall be
holy . . . The profane is now regarded as a preliminary
stage of the holy; it is the not-yet-hallowed. Human
life is destined to be hallowed in its natural form. 'God
dwells where man lets him in!' The hallowing of man
means this 'letting in.' Basically the holy in our world
is what is open to God, as the profane is what is closed
off from Him, and hallowing is the event of opening
out . . ."

To Hallow the Everyday

This is why, according to one of the Rabbis of the
Talmud, the most important verse in the Bible is the
one from the Book of Proverbs, "Know Him in all thy
ways." The word to emphasize in this verse is *all*.
"Know Him in *all* thy ways." This means that we can
"know" God—that is, find Him and serve Him—not
only in the Synagogue or on the Sabbath, but in every
act, in every word, and in every place. It all depends
how we act and how we speak. It all depends on
whether or not we hallow that part of our life. Thus,
we may serve God by the manner in which we speak to
our wife, cast our ballot, fill out our income tax return
or treat our employee. In each case we serve Him by

hallowing the deed we perform, by making it a holy deed. We hallow the everyday by performing each deed so that it becomes a means of serving God. When there is love and devotion between husband and wife, marriage is hallowed; when we vote for the ability and integrity of a man and not the favors he may grant us, we hallow our country; when we deal fairly with our employee, we hallow our business. The duty of the Jew is to lift up all of life to God, *to hallow the everyday*, so that all of life becomes holy.

Indeed, it must be with the everyday, Judaism teaches, that we begin our task of hallowing. If we were to ask Christianity the question: how does a human being become holy, what is the mysterious process through which he attains this exalted quality, we would probably be told: by having the right feeling or thought, by possessing the proper creed or belief. Judaism would agree that feelings and beliefs are essential to holiness, but it would assert that the struggle for holiness on the part of a human being does not *begin* there (nor should it end there for that matter). Judaism is not a one-day-a-week religion, nor does it concern itself only with prayer or Synagogue or ritual, nor does it limit itself to catechisms. On the contrary, its great claim, as expressed throughout the entire range of its literature from the Torah to the latest responsum, is that it must encompass the entirety of a man's being; that it is, in fact, a way of life, affecting all of one's days or none of them, relevant to one's total manner of living or to none of it, just as concerned with the seeming trivialities as with the exalted aspects of one's existence. Indeed, it would assert that it is precisely with these seeming trivialities, these common, everyday actions of ours which are matter-of-fact and habitual and apparently inconsequential that we must commence, in order to create the holy man. And what is more common, more ordinary, more seemingly trivial and inconsequential than the process of eating? It is precisely here that Judaism would have us begin—with the everyday—claiming that it is more significant to learn how to prepare and eat our food than to reflect on a dogma, more important to say *ha-motzi* over a piece of bread than to memorize a creed. Make something fine and decent out of the common practice of eating and you will have achieved more than reading a whole library of books on theology. Man, Judaism seems to teach, is not so much what he *thinks* as what he *does*. Indeed, it would claim, proper thinking may well follow proper doing. Attitudes often derive from activities.[2]

Now we can better understand what the mitzvah of Kashrut is attempting to achieve and can see it in its proper context. We are commanded to be a holy people. "Thou shalt be holy for I the Lord thy God am holy." "Thou shalt be a kingdom of priests and a holy nation." Israel is commanded to be holy; again and again commanded to be holy. But how do we become holy? We become holy by making holy, by hallowing. We become holy by hallowing that which is not yet holy, the profane, the everyday. And it is through observing the mitzvot that we are able to hallow and be hallowed. That is the purpose of the mitzvot. Thus before performing any mitzvah we are bidden to recite a blessing which begins: Blessed art Thou O Lord our

God, King of the world Who hast *hallowed us by Thy mitzvot. . . . (Barukh Atah Adonai Elohenu Melekh Ha-olam Asher Kid'shanu B'mitzvotav. . . .)* Thus the mitzvah of Kashrut was given to Israel in order that they become holy. Israel is commanded to hallow the act of eating, and through this making holy, become holy. Judaism teaches us to hallow every aspect of life through fulfilling the mitzvot. The mitzvah of Kashrut helps us hallow the act of eating.

It is no simple achievement, however, this ennobling of our way of eating. It is a function we have in common with the animals. And there are many who are not greatly different from animals in this respect; they approach it with the same gluttony and coarseness and the same constant concern. Their meals are often vulgar and disgusting. To sit at their table is an ordeal. To hear as the central topic of conversation their discussion of food as served at this or that club, this or that restaurant, this or that party, of the need for dieting and the helpless habit of overeating, is appalling. The descriptions we possess of Roman banquets and the revolting excesses indulged in there certainly remind one of animals. Our modern displays may be somewhat more sophisticated but are not really different in essence. The pagan glorification of elemental needs is still very much with us. Thus, since man is an animal and eating is a bodily function which he has in common with the animal, he may likewise approach his food as an animal—the only thought in mind being how best to satisfy his desires. That is one attitude, the pagan attitude. Conversely, the classical Christian attitude to the problem of food would lie in the denial of the body and all its desires as so many necessary evils which must be tolerated. For it is not the body but the soul which matters, not this world but the world to come. Man is a sinful creature and cannot curb his lust; he is an animal and cannot obey God's law. Therefore the enjoyment of food is often looked upon by Christianity as sinful. Therefore the rigid manner of fasts which the church prescribes and the asceticism which has characterized the main stream of Christianity down to this very day.

Judaism, too, has a place for fasting among its tenets. But it does not see this as a solution to the problem of satisfying the desire for food. Thus we are not only commanded *to fast* on Yom Kippur; we are likewise commanded *to eat* on the day before Yom Yippur. As if to emphasize this, the sages wrote, "If one eats and drinks on the ninth day of Tishri (the day before Yom Kippur), it is as if he would fast on both the ninth *and* tenth days of Tishri." To this a later rabbi wisely remarked: "Thus we are taught that while it is difficult *to fast* for the sake of heaven, it is even more difficult *to eat* for the sake of heaven." Neither the glorification of the elemental drive for food as characterized by Paganism nor the ascetic view of eating as a necessary evil as characterized by classical Christianity. (One extreme has regularly caused a move of the pendulum to the other extreme in history. The reader may judge for himself at which point in the pendulum's swing we find ourselves today.)

Judaism teaches a third way. It says that God created the world and made man in His own image, that He has given man the power to discover God's will and to obey it, and that man's task, therefore, is neither to escape from the world nor to worship it as it is, but with Torah and the mitzvot to fulfill God's dream for His creation. It says we have the power to hallow the act of eating, that we can find a way of ennobling and raising this prosaic act which will lend it meaning and significance, an aspect of holiness, that we may even succeed in transforming it into a means of serving God. For man is not merely an animal, even a *rational* animal, as Aristotle would have it, an animal with a mind; he is better defined as a *religious* animal—an animal, yes, with all the functions and frailties of animals, but a "religious" animal, one which has the wonderful power to take his animal functions and turn them into something holy. The glory of man is his power to hallow. We do not live to eat; we eat to live. Even the act of eating can be sanctified; even the act of eating can become a means for achieving holiness.

Kashrut, therefore, may be defined as a part of Judaism's attempt to hallow the act of eating by teaching us reverence for life.

Eating Meat a Divine Compromise

How does Kashrut hallow the act of eating?

Kashrut teaches, first of all, that the eating of meat is itself a sort of *compromise*. To many it will come as a surprise that Adam, the first man, was not permitted to eat meat. Yet we have only to look closely at the Biblical text to see that this was surely the case.

> And God created man in his own image, in the image of God created He him; male and female created

He them. And God blessed them; and God said unto them: "Be fruitful and multiply, and replenish the earth and subdue it; and have dominion over the fish of the sea, and over the fowl of the air, and over every living thing that creepeth upon the earth." And God said: "Behold, I have given you every herb yielding seed, which is upon the face of all the earth, and every tree, in which is the fruit of a tree yielding seed—to you it shall be for food!" (Gen. 1:27-29)

Thus Adam, the perfect man, as an inhabitant of the Garden of Eden, which represents the divine order of creation, the perfect, ideal society, is limited to fruits and vegetables. He is clearly meant to be a vegetarian. No mention of animals is made here as his food, only "every herb yielding seed" and "every tree in which is the fruit of a tree yielding seed." Not until we come to the story of Noah is meat permitted to be eaten.

And God blessed Noah and his sons, and said unto them: "Be fruitful and multiply, and replenish the earth. And the fear of you and the dread of you shall be upon every beast of the earth, and upon every fowl of the air, and upon all wherewith the ground teemeth, and upon all the fishes of the sea: into your hand are they delivered. *Every moving thing that liveth shall be for you; as the green herb have I given you all. Only flesh with the life thereof, which is the blood thereof, shall ye not eat!*" (Gen. 9: 1-4)

Adam is forbidden meat; Noah is permitted it. Why? What took place between the time of Adam and Noah to bring about this change? The answer is simple: sin. The law for Adam and the law for Noah both represent man: Adam in the Garden of Eden in his ideal state, Noah outside the Garden of Eden in his real state. Adam was not satisfied to live in the paradisal society. He rebelled against God and turned away from him. He wanted the flesh of living creatures for his food and was prepared to kill to obtain it. And so it was with his descendants. Man ideally should not eat meat, for to eat meat a life must be taken, an animal must be put to death. But man will eat meat. It is his desire and, perhaps, too, his need.

Just as at the beginning of time, in the perfect society as symbolized by the Garden of Eden, there was no eating of meat, so at the end of time, in the perfect society as described by the prophet Isaiah, there will be a return to the original state.

And the wolf shall dwell with the lamb
And the leopard shall lie down with the kid;
And the calf and the young lion and the fatling together;
And a little child shall lead them
And the cow and the bear shall feed;
Their young ones shall lie down together;
And the lion shall eat straw like the ox . . .
They shall not hurt nor destroy
In all My holy mountain;

For all the earth shall be full of the knowledge of
  the Lord,
As the waters cover the sea. (Isaiah 11:6,7,9)

Included in the prophet's description of the future
perfect society where all conflict within nature will
give way to peace and harmony is the fact that the lion
shall no longer live on the flesh of other beasts but like
the ox eat the growth of the field. And can we, therefore, not draw the inference that if the carnivorous
animal will disappear at the end of time, how much
more so the carnivorous man? If blood-thirsty animals
will themselves no longer devour other animals but
live on fruits and vegetables and even straw, how much
more so man? Man too, then, in the future time will
no longer eat meat. "The biblical account of the
scheme of human destiny represents it as a temporal
process with creation and the paradisal state at the
beginning and redemption in the Kingdom of God at
the end. In between is history." (Herberg) At the
"beginning" and at the "end" man is, thus, in his ideal
state, herbivorous. His life is not maintained at the
expense of the life of the beast. In "history" which
takes place here and now, and in which man, with all
his frailties and relativities, lives and works out his
destiny, he may be carnivorous.

Human consumption of meat, which means the
taking of an animal life, has constantly posed a religious problem to Judaism, even when it has accepted
the necessity of it. The Rabbis of the Talmud were
aware of the distinction between man's ideal and his
real condition, regarding food. Referring to Deut.

12:20, they said: "The Torah teaches a lesson in moral conduct, that man shall not eat meat unless he has a special craving for it, and shall eat it only occasionally and sparingly."[3] "Only one who studies Torah may eat meat, but one who does not study Torah is forbidden to eat meat."[4] "Once Rabbi Judah the Prince sat and taught Torah before an assembly of Babylonian Jews at Sepphoris, and a calf being led to the slaughter passed before him. It sought to hide itself in his cloak and began to cry, as if to say: 'Save me!' 'What can I do,' said Rabbi Judah, 'since it is for this that you were created?' It was therefore decreed in heaven that because he had no compassion, sufferings should come upon him. One day a weasel ran past his daughter and she wanted to kill it. He said to her, 'Let it be, for it is written, "His mercies are over all His works." ' So it was decreed in heaven that because he had pity, pity shall be shown to him. And his sufferings ceased."[5]

The Rabbis' awareness of the problem is again implied—in their discussion of Biblical traditions—in the manner in which they distinguish between *b'sar kodshim*, "holy meat," that which was first offered in the Tabernacle by the Israelites and only then permitted to be eaten, and *b'sar chulin*, "profane meat," that which was eaten even though it had not first been brought to the Tabernacle. This latter meat—*b'sar chulin*, "profane meat"—was permitted to the people after they had left the wilderness and entered the Land of Israel. It is, however, the term they give to this profane meat which is striking. They call it *b'sar ta'avah*, "meat of lust" or "meat of luxury," after the passage in Deut. 12:20.[6]

When the Lord thy God shall enlarge thy border, as
He hath promised thee, and thou shalt say: "I will
eat flesh," because thy soul lusteth to eat flesh; thou
mayest eat flesh, after the lusting of thy soul. If the
place which the Lord thy God shall choose to put
His name there shall be too far from thee, then thou
shalt kill of thy herd and of thy flock, which the
Lord hath given thee, as I have commanded thee,
and thou shalt eat within thy gates, after all the lusting of thy soul . . . Only be steadfast in not eating
the blood; for the blood is the life; and thou shalt
not eat the life with the flesh. Thou shalt not eat it.
Thou shalt pour it out upon the earth as water.
Thou shalt not eat it; that it may go well with thee,
and with thy children after thee, when thou shalt do
that which is right in the eyes of the Lord." (Deut.
12:20-21, 23-24)

The permission to eat meat is thus seen to be a
compromise, *a divine concession to human weakness
and human need.* The Torah, as it were, says: "I would
prefer that you abstain from eating meat altogether,
that you subsist on that which springs forth from the
earth, for to eat meat the life of an animal must be
taken and that is a fearful act. But since you are not
perfect men and your world is neither a Garden of
Eden nor the Kingdom of God, since your desires
cannot be stopped nor your nutritional requirements
altered, they must at least be controlled; since you will
eat meat and since, perhaps you need to eat meat, you
may eat it, but with one restriction—that you have
reverence for the life that you take." "The flesh with

the soul thereof, which is the blood thereof, shall ye not eat." (Gen. 9:4)

Reverence for the Life We Take

We are permitted to eat meat, but we must learn to have reverence for the life we take. It is part of the process of hallowing which Kashrut proclaims. *Reverence for Life*, teaching an awareness of what we are about when we engage in the simple act of eating flesh, is the constant lesson of the laws of Kashrut. Let us see how this is so.

Sh'chitah, the manner of slaughter. "Thou shalt kill of thy herd and thy flock which the Lord hath given thee, as I have commanded thee." (Deut. 12:21) This is the Biblical source for laws of *Sh'chitah* which are found in the Talmud and probably go back to Biblical times. The laws of *Sh'chitah* provide the most humane method of slaughtering animals. Great care is exercised that the knife to be used must be regularly examined before and after it is used to determine that it is perfectly smooth, without a notch that might tear the flesh. The cut severs the arteries to the head of the animal, thereby stopping circulation to the head and rendering the animal unconscious of all pain. This is not true when the animal is only stunned by a blow. The one who slaughters the animal, the *Shochet*, must be carefully chosen. He not only must slaughter the animal according to Jewish law but is obliged to examine its internal organs to make certain the animal was not diseased. Among non-Jews such positions in slaughterhouses are held, for the most part, by the lowest elements of society—tough, crude men. With

Jews it is otherwise. The *Shochet* must be both a learned and pious person. He must pass an examination attesting to his thorough knowledge of the laws of *Sh'chitah*. He must be a man of piety and is obliged to recite a blessing before he executes his duties, ever reminding him of the nature of his labor, that this whole process is but a "divine concession." Thus he is prevented from becoming brutalized by the manner of his work. ". . . Thou shalt kill of thy herd and thy flock which the Lord hath given thee, as I have commanded thee . . ." (Deut. 12:21); that is, we may slaughter an animal for food, but only "as I have commanded thee." Thus *Sh'chitah* teaches reverence for life.

"The commandment concerning the killing of animals is necessary," writes Maimonides in a similar vein, "because the natural food of man consists of vegetables and of the flesh of animals; the best meat is that of animals permitted to be used as food. No doctor has any doubts about this. Since, therefore, the desire of procuring good food necessitates the slaying of animals, the Law enjoins that the death of the animal should be the easiest. It is not allowed to torment the animal by cutting the throat in a clumsy manner, by poleaxing, or by cutting off a limb whilst the animal is alive. It is also prohibited to kill an animal with its young on the same day (Lev. 22:28), in order that people should be restrained and prevented from killing the two together in such a manner that the young is slain in the sight of the mother; for the pain of the animals under such circumstances is very great. There is no difference in this case between the pain of man and the pain of other living beings, since the love and tenderness of the mother for her young ones . . . exists not only in man but in most living beings."[7]

Kashering, the removal of blood. Through the process of *Kashering* the blood is removed from the meat. It is not enough that the animal must be killed in the most humane way, that the life of the animal is taken with care and concern, but even the *symbol* of life, the blood, must be removed. "Only be steadfast in not eating the blood; for the blood is the life, and thou shalt not eat the blood with the flesh." (Deut. 12:23-25; also Lev. 17:11; cf. I Sam. 14:32-34) To remove the blood is the purpose of the laws of *Kashering.* There is no clearer visible symbol of life than blood. To spill blood is to bring death. To inject blood is often to save life. The removal of blood which Kashrut teaches is one of the most powerful means of making us constantly aware of the concession and compromise which the whole act of eating meat, in reality, is. Again it teaches us reverence for life.

Limitation of animals to be eaten. Because we are permitted to eat meat only as a compromise, a divine concession to human weakness and need, animals which are *n'velah* (that which dieth of itself) or *t'refah* (that which is killed by another animal) are forbidden. Such animals have not been killed according to the Law, which procedure alone renders them permissible for food, since it alone attempts to reverence the life it takes. And only animals so treated may be eaten. Animals found to be diseased upon examination by the *Shochet* are declared *t'refah.* Furthermore, only tame, domestic animals which are herbivorous can be eaten. The especially fierce species of carnivorous fowl, such as the hawk and eagle, are forbidden.

The Larger Meaning of Reverence for Life

The lesson of reverence for life which the laws of Kashrut teach has by no means been accepted in our world where life, animal and human, seems to be the cheapest of all commodities.

Only recently a discussion of the morality of hunting appeared in a well known magazine. One writer, the distinguished critic, Joseph Wood Krutch, commented that ordinary killers "are selfish and unscrupulous, but their deeds are not gratuitously evil. The killer for sport has no such comprehensible motive. He prefers death to life, darkness to light. He gets nothing except the satisfaction of saying, 'something which wanted to live is dead. There is that much less vitality, consciousness, and, perhaps, joy in the universe. I am the Spirit that Denies.' When a man wantonly destroys one of the works of man we call him Vandal. When he wantonly destroys one of the works of God we call him Sportsman." The zoologist, H. E. Anthony, who defends hunting in the same discussion, admits "that a basic inconsistency underlies the shooting of game . . .: no one will deny that there is an inconsistency in cherishing a beautiful dog for many years and going out every fall to shoot an equally beautiful deer. But, so far as we know, there is no escape from the tension of inconsistencies of which life consists."

The reason why the world has never adopted the

opinion of a Mr. Krutch is because there has always been a Mr. Anthony to throw up his hands in despair and say that there is nothing we can do about it, that man may be considerate to animals one moment and take joy in destroying them the next moment, that the feeling of kindness is countered by the urge to destroy: that there is a killer instinct in man which cannot be controlled. He might point to the so-called national pastimes of cockfighting and bullfighting which draw hundreds and thousands of spectators eager to see a bird torn to pieces or an animal pierced with a blade. And what of boxing in our own country, he might add. If you watch the average crowd at a prizefight carefully, you will observe that when the fighters dance about, feint and block, be they ever so skilled in the art of boxing, the crowd is bored and grows restless. They want to see some action; they want to see a "killing."

The Jew is unable to look upon the sport of hunting simply as an opportunity to get out into the open air, flex his muscles and "renew his contact with nature." He views the deliberate shooting of an animal for no reason other than "sport" with utter abhorrence and sees in it the aggressive instinct in man coming to the fore. He knows that in the repeated act of killing, man himself may become a killer. Judaism recognizes this as a very real danger which confronts man. But it neither offers pious platitudes of condemnation nor does it confess helplessness. It has devised the laws of Kashrut as a habitual system of spiritual discipline which trains the Jew each and every day to have reverence for life, even though life must be taken to provide

him with food. By restricting the kinds of animals
which may be eaten, and providing for a humane
manner of slaughter and a trained slaughterer, we are
prevented from becoming brutalized by the killing of
animals for our food.

Reverence for life which Kashrut stands for finds
rich expression in Judaism. Many laws in the Bible,
for example, teach kindness to animals. Animals are
allowed to rest on the Sabbath (Exodus 23:12).
Ploughing with a bull and a donkey harnessed together is forbidden because they were not equal in
strength and the weaker would suffer in trying to keep
up with the stronger (Deut. 22:10). If a man finds a
nest of birds, he cannot take the mother bird and the
young; he first has to send away the mother to spare
her feelings (Deut. 22:6). While treading out the corn,
the ox (or any other animal) cannot be muzzled
(Deut. 25:4). When an animal is born, it is not to be
taken away from its mother for at least seven days. An
animal and its young must not be killed on the same
day, lest through thoughtlessness the young is killed
before the eyes of the parent (Levit. 22:26-33). The
Talmudic phrase, "*tzaar baal chayim*" (cruelty to any
living creature), which is considered a crime, has become a virtual folk expression among the Jewish people. Before one is permitted to sit down at his table to
eat a meal, the Talmud says, his animals must first have
been fed. Although the prohibition of not eating the
limb of a living animal was one of the seven Noachidic
laws, laws which the Torah proclaimed for all mankind, "today," H. Lowe points out, "eels are still
skinned alive, cod is crimped and lobsters are boiled

unpithed. It is remarkable that Jews did not kill animals for sport. Fish had to be netted. Mr. William Radcliffe in his book, *Fishing From Earliest Times*, blames Jews for lacking the sporting spirit. They caught fish by net; they did not play them with the rod. This is perfectly true. The word 'hook' occurs in the Bible only as a metaphor of cruelty, or as an instrument used by foreigners."

It is of significance to note that while the law requires a special benediction—"Blessed art Thou, O Lord our God, King of the Universe, who hast kept us in life, and hast preserved us, and hast enabled us to reach this season"—to be recited by a Jew upon putting on a piece of clothing for the first time, it makes an exception in the case of shoes, because they are made of leather. The life of an animal had to be taken to fashion them.

This, in fact, is the reason given in the *Siddur, Haminhagim,* for the prohibition against wearing shoes on Yom Kippur. "Rabbi Moses Isserles wrote: 'It is the custom to say to a person putting on a new garment, "May you wear it out and get a new one." There are some who write that one ought not to say this about shoes or clothing which are made from the skin of animals (even if unclean), for if that were the case, it would seem as though the animal were being killed to make a garment, and it is written, 'His tender mercies are over all His works.' Rabbi Moses Isserles also wrote that he who is slaughtering an animal for the first time ought to recite the blessing *shehecheyanu* when he covers the blood of the animal, not when he slaughters it; for he is injuring a living thing. Therefore, how can a man put on shoes, a piece of clothing for which it is necessary to kill a living thing, on Yom Kippur, which is a day of grace and compassion, when it is written, 'His tender mercies are over all His works'?"

One more word needs to be said about the lesson of reverence for life which the laws of Kashrut teach, perhaps the most important word of all. We have remarked that man possesses an aggressive tendency which the laws of Kashrut attempt to tame and control. But the matter does not end there, for the urge to kill in man, once aroused, may not stop with animals. Where does one draw the line between killing an animal and killing a human? To stalk a deer and hunt him down or to stalk a human being and hunt him down is not greatly different.

"The sight of blood, the rattle of death and the glassy stare contrive to dampen the joy of the first kill, if not to leave the initiate sick to his stomach. To kill for the first time may be an ordeal. Thereafter, however, the protest of the conscience is stifled: after repeated performances, compassion takes flight, love goes into hiding and other emotions fill the vacuum. The prospect of the hunt produces an exultation which henceforth is extended to the prospect of the kill. In the history of man, hunting began as a necessity: in self-defense or for food and clothing. But the means became an end: hunting for sport, to kill for the sake of killing, for the sheer pleasure of killing.

"Here is where the teachers of Judaism detected a danger to human society, claiming that he who brings death to a living thing willfully and wantonly is liable, under certain conditions, to bring death to the highest living thing, man. They spoke from personal experience. For they and their fellow Jews lived for centuries as lieges of hunter-sportsmen, and were not infrequently tortured, maimed and murdered with the same skills perfected in the hunt. Furthermore, in the course of their historical experiences, they saw the identical hunting skills applied to the greatest hunt of all—human warfare. And because they saw that war also was governed by gentlemenly rules—whether the Treuga Dei of the middle ages or the rules of the Geneva Conference of the past century—they felt justified in identifying war with the hunt, except that now the entire earth became the hunter's domain and its human occupants his most prized game."† Once the sense of reverence for life has been dulled, the conscience is blunted and the divine image in man obscured. The beast within him that has been chained and hidden then emerges with all his fearful power.

Is this not precisely what we have witnessed in our own generation and is this not the very danger that threatens the world today—that those who have no reverence for life will destroy mankind? Furthermore, is not the destruction of human life perhaps the most popular theme of the daily "games" which our children indulge in, gun in their hand and murder in their eye? Is not the destruction of human life the stock in trade of almost every comic book, movie or television program? The results of a recent study showed that

†Jacob Milgrom, "Jews Are Not Hunters," unpublished manuscript. I have drawn upon this provocative article at length in this section ("Reverence for the Life We Take"). Much of the material in the next session ("Why Ritual?") was likewise taken from the Milgrom essay.

over six thousand murders occurred on the television screens throughout the nation on a single day! This is the education our children receive two or three or more hours each day of the week. The incidence of juvenile delinquency—among which is juvenile murder—can be traced, in part, to the education to destroy which the average child cannot help but soak up from his daily games, the mass entertainment media and, even, the daily newspapers. We are living in an age when six million Jews could perish without great concern on the part of the world, because man's sense of horror has been blunted; an age which has invented a means of burning millions—the crematorium; a means of blowing up millions—the atomic bomb; and a term for annihilating an entire people—genocide. Was there ever an age which needed more the lesson of reverence for life?

There is hardly a more powerful or more effective means of teaching this lesson than the proper observance of the mitzvah of Kashrut, which is a daily education throughout one's entire lifetime, observed in the privacy of each individual home. *Kashering* and *Sh'chitah*, not to eat blood and a humane manner of slaughter, far from being outmoded are among the most up-to-date and relevant laws of our tradition. Indeed, if a new religion were to be created today, such injunctions might well be among the first to be promulgated for the needs of Twentieth Century man.

Why Ritual?

But is a specific ritual necessary to teach this lesson? Let us consider the matter. Thinkers today are concerned about how best to teach reverence for life, not only as a noble quality engendering kindness to animals but as a means of preserving our very civilization. Albert Schweitzer, the famous musician-theologian-physician, wrote thousands of pages about the solemn necessity of feeling reverence for life, which to him is the fundamental concept of humanity. Few people, it must be confessed, paid attention to him. When he left fame and fortune in Europe at the height of his success and settled in darkest Africa to found and personally direct a hospital in order to put to practice his belief and thereby bring it more to the attention of the world through his bold example, the number of his followers grew, and at the age of eighty he even received the Nobel Prize. But Schweitzer knows that with all his effort, he has succeeded in changing the thinking of only a handful of people and the lives of even less, and that when he dies, sad to say, what he stood for will probably die with him. Such is the way of man. Judaism, however, has always taught that words and human examples are good but not good enough. It claims to possess a surer way of bringing its great teachings into the heart and mind of every Jew. It is the way of the mitzvah. Jewish law, which is composed of the mitzvot, takes the great teachings of the Bible and fixes them into a regular pattern of observance which fashions a meaningful way of life, and through habitual repetition of this pattern and walking upon this way a higher kind of human being is created. The mitzvah of Kashrut is an eloquent example of this. Thus the reverence for life which Judaism teaches is not dependent on any one man or his admonitions, be his life ever so noble or his writings ever so wise. Kashrut is a systematic means of educating and refining the conscience of those who observe it from early age to death which continues in every age and in every country wherever there is a Jewish family and a Jewish home.

The observance of Kashrut by the people of Israel has helped to do precisely this for them over the centuries, for to teach reverence for animal life is, all the more, to teach reverence for human life. The Jews are called *"rachmanim b'ne rachmanim,* merciful ones and the children of merciful ones."* The Talmud teaches that "man should rather be among the persecuted than the persecutors," and the Biblical reference to support this which is referred to, is one of the laws of Kashrut: that only animals which do not prey on other animals, such as the lamb or the cow, could be brought as sacrifices to the Temple. Have the laws of Kashrut contributed to the merciful nature of the Jewish people? "Consider the one circumstance," wrote A. Leroy-Beaulieu, "that no Jewish mother ever killed a chicken with her own hand, and you will understand why homicide is so rare among the Jews."

The majority of mankind agrees with the oft-repeated verse from the New Testament—"Not that which goeth into the mouth defileth a man; but that which cometh out of the mouth." But Judaism knows that what goes into the mouth can also defile a man, and thus it has created the system of Kashrut which has worked an untold good for the people of Israel throughout the centuries. The laws of Kashrut—which forbid the eating of blood, limit the number of animals which may be eaten and provides for a humane method of slaughter and a specially trained slaughterer—have helped to attain Judaism's goal of hallowing the act of eating by reminding the Jew that the life of the animal is sacred and may be taken to provide him with food only under these fixed conditions. From this he learns reverence for life, both animal and human.

Other people engage in diets for their bodies. We have created a diet for the soul. If the first is understandable, why not the second?

How We Eat

I remarked above that Kashrut—which teaches us that *the eating of meat is a compromise to human weakness and need and that we must therefore have reverence for the life of the animal which we take*—is only a *part* of Judaism's way of sanctifying the act of eating. This must be emphasized. Kashrut cannot be understood by itself; it is a part of something larger. Kashrut alone, therefore, is not enough. It is not only *what* we eat but just as much *how* we eat. And one cannot deal with the one without dealing with the other.

The Talmud says that the table upon which we eat is like the altar of the Temple. The whole process of eating is thus changed into a richly beautiful ceremony. We are bidden to wash our hands before breaking bread not simply to cleanse them—indeed, even if they already are quite clean, water must be poured upon them in the prescribed manner—but because the priests washed their hands before they offered a sacrifice. Salt is sprinkled over the bread with which we begin our meal, because salt was put upon the ancient sacrifice. And between the blessing over the washing of the hands and the blessing over the bread no word is spoken. Then the prayer, "Blessed art Thou, O Lord our God, King of the Universe, who bringest forth bread from the earth," reminding us from whose goodness and lovingkindness our food comes is recited. After the meal, Grace is said, thanking God for having given us our meal and blessing the members of the household. While Grace is recited, the knife is covered, because no knife was allowed to come upon the ancient altar, for the knife was a sign of war and the altar a sign of peace. During the meal we are told to speak words of Torah so that the children and ourselves should be nourished not only by God's food but by His word as well. Someone has remarked, and wisely too, that a child is as much educated by what he hears at his table as what he hears in his school room. "R. Simeon said: 'If three have eaten at a table and have spoken there no word of Torah, it is as if they had eaten of sacrifices to dead idols. . . . But if three have eaten at a table and have spoken there words of Torah, it is as if they had eaten at the table of the Lord.' "

Today we have no Temple in Jerusalem, no altar there, no sacrifices, no priests to minister. But in their stead we have something even greater. For every home can be a Temple, every table an altar, every meal a sacrifice and every Jew a priest. And what was formerly an animal function, a meaningless, mechanical behavior, is suddenly transformed into an elaborate ritual full of mystery and meaning.

Thus Judaism takes something which is common and ordinary, which is everyday and prosaic and ennobles it, raising it to unexpected heights, informing it with profound significance by laws of *what* to eat and *how* to eat, by teaching us that every act of life can be hallowed, even the act of eating. Abraham Heschel gave classic expression to this thought when he wrote that "perhaps the essential message of Judaism is that in doing the finite, we can perceive the infinite." In eating a slice of bread, we can discover God; in drinking a cup of wine we can sanctify the Sabbath; in preparing a piece of meat we can learn something of the reverence of life.

And so it is that in hallowing our eating *we* become hallowed, in making our habits holy *we* become holy. A whole people becomes holy—"a kingdom of priests and a holy nation"; an entire nation set apart for His service. Judaism is a way of life, which encompasses the kitchen and the dining room as well as the Synagogue. Not the glorification of man's elemental drives as in Paganism nor the unnatural subjugation of them as in classical Christianity and the Eastern religions, but the hallowing of them, the raising of them up to God, is the view of Judaism. The glory of man, it teaches, is his power to hallow. By means of this hallowing, he not only overcomes the beast within him but even surpasses the angels.

Concerning Abraham's receiving the three angels and preparing a meal for them, it is written, "And he stood *above* them,[8] under the tree, and they did eat." (Gen. 18:8) Puzzled by this verse, a disciple of Rabbi Zusya of Hanipol asked him if it was not strange that

Scripture should say that the man stood *above* the angels.

No, Rabbi Zusya explained. It was not strange at all. The angels are superior to man, but man is also superior to the angels. The angels are superior to man because they are pure and not a part of the natural world. Man is superior to the angels because, though he is a part of nature, he possesses the power to hallow and raise up to God the common, natural acts of which the angels know nothing. This verse is an example of that. The angels have no need of food and thus, even though they are pure, they are ignorant of the manner in which to hallow the act of eating. But Abraham was a man who knew that even by the way in which we approach our food, we can serve the Almighty. Thus, in this case when he invited them to his table for a meal, Scripture speaks the truth: he stood *above* them.

The man who finds his way to God in the midst of the world is greater than the angels. The angels may be pure because they are apart from our world; they come from heaven and are innocent of the tasks, the problems and vexations that confront man. They are static; they neither rise nor fall in their everlasting splendour. But man comes from earth as well as heaven; he possesses a body as well as a soul; he has evil thoughts as well as good ones; he knows passion and greed as well as justice and mercy. He is never static but rises and falls, is capable of turning into a beast or the most glorious of creatures. Man can be purer than the angels because he—and only he—is called upon to raise earth to heaven. Man can rise higher than the angels because his task is greater than theirs—to hallow all of life: to conduct his business with honesty, to be gentle with his wife and children, to fight for good government, to treat his fellowman as he would be treated, to curb jealousy and desire, to act in such a way that all his deeds become holy deeds, all his actions holy actions, even the commonest of them. Abraham stood above the angels because he knew something utterly unknown to them, namely, that eating may be hallowed by the thoughts, the intentions, the manners, the blessings and the preparations of the eater.

II

THE PROBLEM OF DOING

At the beginning of this essay it was stated that the decline of Kashrut observance in our time stemmed from two causes: lack of proper knowledge about it and lack of the will to do it. The first subject has, albeit briefly and inadequately, been dealt with. I have tried to demonstrate how Kashrut is part of Judaism's attempt to hallow the common act of eating and, therefore, why buying from a Kosher butcher who sells meat slaughtered by a *Shochet*, removing blood from the meat in preparing it for the table, saying a blessing before and after meals—why all this has relevance and meaning, lending holiness to a mechanical function and helping to produce a holy people. It is a matter of correct knowledge, of replacing false understanding with proper understanding, a matter of mind.

But there is something else involved in the problem of Kashrut, and that is the matter of *will*. The practice of Kashrut has to do with our will to live as Jews, with a decision that requires sacrifice and commitment, with a state of mind that is clear and decided. That is why the decline in Kashrut observance is so disturbing. It is not only a question of understanding—though this is central to the whole issue—but also one of determination, of the will to be a Jew.

To Be Holy Means To Be Set Apart

This second consideration, it should be noted, is likewise implied in the meaning of the Hebrew word for holiness, *K'dushah*, which the Bible constantly associates with the Dietary Laws. We have already said that the purpose of Kashrut was holiness and that holiness meant *hallowing*, in this case the hallowing of the act of eating. But the Hebrew word for holiness, *K'dushah*, has another meaning as well. It also means *to be set apart*. To be holy also means to be set apart. "I am the Lord your God, who have *set you apart* from the nations. Ye shall therefore separate between the clean beast and the unclean." (Lev. 20:24-25) The prohibition of certain kinds of fish or the separation of milk and meat, which is the outstanding characteristic of the Jewish kitchen and involves a goodly percentage of the laws of Kashrut, functions mainly to set us apart from non-Jews by providing us with a Jewish cuisine, Jewish kitchen and a Jewish table.[9]

Hallowing the act of eating is an acceptable concept to most people, but being set apart from others by virtue of this hallowing is not so acceptable. To many the whole idea of a democratic society in which ghetto walls are broken down and all peoples and faiths mingle freely and easily militates against such an impregnable food barrier as Kashrut. It is looked upon as a deterrent to good interfaith relations and was, therefore, one of the first parts of the Law which the early German Reformers dropped in their attempt to eliminate the non-universalistic aspects of Judaism. Indeed, even those who do keep Kosher homes do not hesitate to part company with these observances once they leave the privacy of their homes. "At home a Jew, in society a man," as the old Haskalah adage had it. Edmond Fleg, the distinguished French author, tells us in his moving autobiography, *Why I Am a Jew*, how, as a young boy, this double standard Kashrut of convenience drove him from his religion. "Once I was taken on a journey by my parents and at the hotel where we dined the fat and the lean were mixed, and cheese was served after meat. Even ham appeared on the table. My parents ate and permitted me to eat of this forbidden dish. Then the food forbidden at home was no longer forbidden when one was away from home? The law was law no longer?" Such inconsistency on the part of the parent is the surest way to guarantee that the next generation will abandon the Dietary Laws altogether. Such double standards can only be retained by virtue of an emotional nostalgia which is rarely, if ever, inherited. Either Kashrut is taken seriously as a means of singling Israel out as a people set apart for the Lord's service, every meal, therefore, being an opportunity to give witness to this fact, a regimen having significance not only in the confines of the home but outside the confines of the home as well, or it is doomed to extinction.

The tremendously alluring power of conformity as described by Riesman and others which sweeps together into the "accepted" pattern all dissident elements, all heterogeneous members, is nothing new to the Jewish people. It is an old ailment, whose bitter pain we have often felt. We call it, however, by a different name: assimilation, the desire to abandon one's distinctiveness and become like those around us. It is a constant temptation to the Jew: to give up the interminable struggle and go along submissively, indistinguishably, passively with the rest of the crowd. Furthermore, the distinction between inner-directed and other-directed persons, which the sociologists now use to describe those who act out of their own resources ("inner"-directed) in contrast to those who suppress their own feelings and conform to the crowd ("other"-directed), is exactly what we mean and have meant for centuries, when, discussing the Jews of Alexandria and Spain and Germany, we spoke of the assimilationists and the non-assimilationists. The only difference today is that the trend toward assimilation, that is, ridding ourselves of distinctive practices, is so much the greater in America because of the paucity of anti-Semitism and the overwhelmingly integrating factors of democracy. All this stands as a wall of protest against the practice of Kashrut, urging conformity, like-acting, like-speaking, like-eating, frowning upon anything in the way of thought or manner which might cause one to stand out from the crowd. Thus, it is not

only a matter of understanding the meaning of Kashrut but also the will to do it that must be considered.

Kashrut in Jewish History

The people of Israel have possessed the will to observe the laws of Kashrut in the past. So strong has
their will been to observe Kashrut that they considered
it worthy of great sacrifice, even, at times, the greatest
sacrifice. Consider for a moment the role which Kashrut has played in our history. At the time of the
Maccabees part of the Greek persecution consisted in
attempting to force the desecration of the Dietary Laws
upon the Jews. The aged scribe Eleazar submitted to
death rather than permit pig's flesh to pass his lips
and is one of the first recorded martyrs of Israel. The
record of the observance of these ritual prescriptions
and of the self-sacrifice that was willingly undertaken
for their sake is closely bound up with the whole
subsequent course of Jewish history. Josephus tells us
of the Essenes who, at the time of the great war against
the Romans, "racked and twisted, burnt and broken,
and made to pass through every instrument of torture,
in order to induce them to blaspheme their lawgiver or
to eat some forbidden thing, they refused to yield to
either demand, nor even once did they cringe to their
persecutors or shed a tear." Philo speaks of similar
episodes in Alexandria. And so, too, in later genera-
tions, under different skies and in different circumstances. It is recounted how the Marranos of Spain
risked their lives to procure meat that was Kosher and
how this detail was considered one of the signs of

heresy by the Inquisition, which sometimes brought them to their death. There is a record even of how certain of them, arrested by the Holy Office, managed to observe the Dietary Laws in the very dungeons in which they were immured. Thus a certain Francisco Maldanado da Silva, who was burned alive in Lima in 1639, refused to touch meat all the long years during which he lay in the condemned cell awaiting his fate; and this is not the only case. The same took place at the time of the Crusades when many Jews were dragged to the baptismal font but nevertheless clung to their ancestral practice. "It is fitting that I should recount their praise," writes a contemporary chronicler, "for whatever they ate. . . . they did at the peril of their lives. They would ritually slaughter animals for food according to the Jewish tradition." (Roth) Miraculous are the tales of Jewish boys who were forcibly taken into the Russian army at a tender age by Czar Nicholas, separated from their families, raised in distant lands as soldiers, beaten and starved to make them abandon their Jewish ways, and who nevertheless refused to eat forbidden food. To this could be added endless tales of spiritual heroism during the period of Nazi persecution of our own time. Apart from all these examples of endangering one's very life, is the day to day sacrifice which our people have made without question, complaint or any claims to heroics, in the ordinary course of their affairs: when they happened to be away from home on a trip or if they lived in a small village and had to travel many miles to purchase Kosher meat or the countless other cases in the ordinary life of the people of Israel when they overcame difficulties in order to fulfill the mitzvah of Kashrut. The weight of Jewish history regarding the Dietary Laws weighs heavy upon us. The Talmud says that those mitzvot for which Israel have had to suffer have thereby become especially dear to them. The mitzvah of Kashrut is undoubtedly included in that group.

Particularism and Universalism

Perhaps we have been selling our Judaism too cheaply of late, pruning it of all seeming unpleasantries, hiding from the American Jew what the real demands of our faith are, candy-coating it, making it sweet to the taste, pleasant to the eyes, something that gives a little brightness and color to whatever kind of man you may happen to be. In a word: peace of mind. The real challenge of tradition is glossed over; the rigorous demands of the Law are rarely mentioned. Instead, those aspects of the tradition are dealt with which will arouse the least objection and the rest studiously ignored. Kashrut is among that portion which is ignored.

The truth is, however, that Judaism does make demands, stern, difficult—almost impossible—demands. Judaism is a strict discipline which has produced—by virtue of intensive and meaningful education and observance over a long period of years a special kind of man and peculiar kind of people. Such results do not come about automatically, from pious platitudes. Our claim is not peace of mind; our claim is that the God of Israel spoke to all mankind through Israel, that we are His messengers to all the world, that the world

depends upon the truth enunciated in our tradition
and that we are the keepers of that heritage for all
mankind. Destroy the people and you destroy that
heritage. For that heritage is not embodied in any book
or idea (as with the Greeks) but in the people's living
reality, the way of life which is tradition. We Jews are
a narrow, nationalistic, self-centered people. There is
no point in denying it. Only read the first part of the
Alenu prayer which is recited at every Jewish service
(except the Reform, which found its particularism too
offensive):

> It is our duty to praise the Lord of all things, to
> ascribe greatness to Him who formed the world in
> the beginning, since He hath not made us like the
> nations of other lands, and hath not placed us like
> other families of the earth, since He hath not as-
> signed unto us a portion as unto them, nor a lot as
> unto all multitude. We bend the knee and offer
> worship and thanks before the supreme King of
> Kings, the Holy One, blessed be He. . . .

The severe particularism of Israel is nowhere better
expressed than in these words. They contain part of
good Jewish doctrine. They declare our separateness,
and our thankfulness for our separateness. But is this
particularism an end in itself? Are we *only* particularistic? The answer to that question is found in the
second paragraph of the very same prayer:

> We therefore hope in Thee, O Lord our God, that
> we may soon behold the glory of Thy might, when
> Thou wilt remove the abominations from the earth

and cause all idolatry to cease. We hope for the day when the world will be perfected under the kingdom of the Almighty, and all mankind will call upon Thy name; when Thou wilt turn unto Thyself all the wicked of the earth. May all the inhabitants of the world perceive and know that unto Thee every knee must bend, every tongue vow loyalty. Before Thee, O Lord our God, may they bow in worship, giving honor unto Thy glorious name. May they all accept the yoke of Thy kingdom and do Thou rule over them speedily and forevermore. For the kingdom is Thine and to all eternity Thou wilt reign in glory; as it is written in Thy Torah; The Lord shall be King over all the earth; on that day the Lord shall be one and His name one.

The loftiest, most universal utterance in our entire liturgy is thus joined to the most particularistic. And what is true of this prayer is true of all of Judaism. Particularism and universalism go hand in hand. This is the message of the Bible and the Talmud, the prophets and the rabbis. We are a small, intensive people which strives through much of its ritual to preserve itself; yet the end of this struggle is not simple self-preservation—why be a Jew and suffer on that account?—but to be a witness to God amidst the follies and miseries of mankind, that the day might come when the world would be perfected under the kingdom of the Almighty, when every knee would bend and every tongue pledge loyalty, when God alone would rule, when He and His name would be one. Particularism and universalism, both are essentials of Judaism.

Destroy one and you destroy both. There have been
times in Jewish history when the universal aspect of
Judaism was almost forgotten, as is the danger in the
land of Israel today. There have been times when the
particularistic aspect of Judaism was almost forgotten,
as is the danger in America today. In either case a
fatal blow will have been leveled at the total Gestalt of
the Jewish faith.

> Ye are My witnesses, saith the Lord;
> And My servant whom I have chosen.
> I the Lord have called thee in righteousness,
> And have taken hold of thy hand,
> And kept thee and set thee for a covenant of the
>   people,
> For a light to the nations;
> To open the blind eyes,
> To bring out the prisoners from the dungeon,
> And them that sit in darkness out of the prison-
>   house.
>
> (Isa.43:10; 42:6-7)

Holiness means *to hallow our lives*, but it also means
to be set apart for the Lord. Thus one of the primary
functions of Kashrut is to distinguish us from others,
to separate us from the nations, to preserve us amidst
the maelstroms of history. This must be said clearly
and unashamedly. And such separation is just as necessary today in America as ever before. The logic involved is clear: if Judaism has a task in the world,
then there must be Jews in the world. Otherwise there
will be no Judaism. But the Jews are a small nation
scattered amongst the peoples. How can they be pre-

vented from being swallowed up and assimilated in the course of the years? Kashrut helps to separate them, to distinguish them and preserve them, to remind them three times a day who they are and what God chose them to stand for, that all their days and hours—not only certain days and certain hours—should be for His sake. A gentile prophet spoke better than he knew when he said of Israel: "Lo, it is a people that shall dwell alone, and shall not be reckoned among the nations." (Num. 23:9)

Kashrut is one of the firmest ramparts of the particularistic aspect of Judaism. It demands sacrifice, self-discipline and determination—but what that is really worthwhile in life does not? It demands the courage to turn our face against the powerful current of conformity that almost overcomes us daily, not only against the gentile world as in the past (that was difficult enough, yet in doing so, one could always feel part of an united people), but against the majority of the *Jewish* world, thus standing witness to God amongst our own nation as well as the "nations." Is this not, however, what the prophet Isaiah—he who spoke of his people as God's "witness" and "servant"—meant when he sang of a "saving remnant" of Israel? Throughout our long history—from Egypt to Palestine to Babylonia to Spain to Germany to America—it has always been that loyal "remnant," not the entire people, which has been faithful to our task and preserved our heritage from generation to generation. Perhaps we should thus describe the Jew who observes Kashrut today as something different from the Riesman categories of "inner-" and "other"-directed. Perhaps we should rather call him "tradition"-directed. It is the weight of the centuries which he carries in his soul that gives him strength, the yoke of the *halakhah*, the "way," which determines his course, the long chain of tradition to which he is bound and to which he yearns to add one more link, that guides his path—while before his eyes remains the glorious vision of the end of time when all nations will be one. Because he says "yes" to the glory and the grandeur of Jewish tradition, he has the courage to say "no" to the world with all its allurements and blandishments, with all its captivating call to conformity. The problem of Kashrut is very much involved with the will to live as a Jew.

To summarize, then, we may say that the goal of Kashrut is holiness, a holy man and a holy nation. It is a part of Judaism's attempt to hallow the common act of eating which is an aspect of our animal nature. It likewise sets us apart from the nations. Thus it achieves its objective, holiness, in these two ways, both of which are implied in the Hebrew word, *Kadosh*: inner hallowing and outer separateness. Finally, Kashrut makes two demands upon the modern Jew: understanding of the mind and commitment of the will. Both are indispensable.

According to Aristotle's pupil Clearchus, his master once had a discourse with a Jew and came away deeply impressed with two things about this people: their admirable philosophy and their strict diet.

Philosophy and diet, thought and practice, inner attitude and outward observance, *agadah* and *halakhah*—this combination has characterized Judaism since earliest times. It is the very essence of the Jewish religion.

THE JEWISH DIETARY LAWS:

A Guide to Observance

Preface

The Dietary Laws are a powerful force within the Jewish way of life. They are designed to increase God-consciousness in Jews, to refine their appetites and desires, and to help them identify with the Jewish people. The laws of kashrut observed in the daily life of the people Israel serve to hallow the everyday and introduce an element of holiness (*kedushah*) every day of the year. By observing these rules of diet, we are made aware of the sovereignty of the divine within our existence, even in such a mundane activity as eating.

The laws of kashrut have undergone a long development within Jewish history. They are basically outlined in the Bible, explained and expanded in ancient rabbinic writing, interpreted and systematized by medieval codifiers and expanded in the thousands of questions and answers (*She'elot U'teshuvot*) found in the correspondence of the great rabbis of every epoch.

Over the years and in varying locales, rabbinic authorities differed in their interpretations of specific laws. Thus, variations in local practice came into being. To cite a famous example: Sephardic Jews eat rice and legumes on Passover; Ashkenazic Jews do not. Ashkenazic Jews, by and large, do not eat the hindquarters of beef; Sephardic Jews do. These local differences have not prevented an overarching unity of purpose. There has always been mutual respect even when there were variations in behavior.

The Dietary Laws have become particularly complex in our modern technological age. We now have to deal with a multitude of new products and processes. New materials are used in the production of utensils, new chemicals are added to basic foods, and new methods of food production raise problems which could not have been foreseen by our forebears.

These new developments make it necessary to constantly reinterpret and reexamine the rules which we have inherited. In the Conservative Movement within Judaism, the task of dealing with new developments is given over to the rabbi of each congregation. He is the religious authority within his community, the *mara d'atra*. The local rabbi, for guidance and advice, frequently looks to the Committee on Jewish Law and Standards of the Rabbinical Assembly. This Committee is vested with the responsibility of making authoritative decisions and offering guidance on matters of Jewish law for the Movement as a whole.

In the pages that follow, we outline the laws of kashrut as they have developed throughout the ages. These are based, of course, on the authoritative codes of Jewish law. We have also consulted experts in food chemistry and production, so that we could apply the rules of kashrut where scientific and technological issues are raised.

Some of the decisions recorded here are not accepted by all authorities on Jewish law, notably decisions about wine, cheese, gelatin, swordfish and sturgeon. This is not a novel situation in the history of Jewish law. There have always been disagreements on various points. What we have indicated is the *predominant* view on questions where there are differences of opinion.

We have attempted to present the observance of kashrut in

its authentic and accurate fashion. We sincerely hope that this will cause Jews to unite in their sacred goal of becoming "a kingdom of priests and a holy people," *mamlekhet kohanim v'goy kadosh.*

A number of individuals have made important contributions to this work. We wish to thank especially Herman Friedman and Gerald Greber of the General Foods Corporation for their kind assistance in preparing the section on chemical additives. Invaluable help was given by Rabbi Wolfe Kelman, Executive Vice-President of the Rabbinical Assembly, and Rabbi Jules Harlow, Director of Publications for the Rabbinical Assembly. For careful review and suggestions, we are grateful to Dr. Morton K. Siegel, Director of Education for the United Synagogue, and Rabbi Joseph Braver, Assistant Director. Rabbi Jose Faur was extremely helpful in elucidating various halakhic issues. Rabbis David Graubart, Ben Zion Bokser, and Benjamin Z. Kreitman reviewed the material and offered important suggestions. Ruth Seldin improved the text with her editorial skills. We are grateful to Mr. Andrew Amsel for his expertise in production. Final responsibility, of course, rests with the authors.

We wish to acknowledge our debt to Rabbi Isaac Klein, of blessed memory, whose pioneering work in the application of halakhic principles to modern issues has been a constant guide to those who wish to know and appreciate Jewish law.

RABBI SEYMOUR SIEGEL

DAVID M. POLLOCK

Observing the Dietary Laws

To observe the Dietary Laws is to adopt not only a philosophy but a lifestyle that influences every activity relating to eating: the choice of foods, the organization of the kitchen, meal planning, and eating away from home.

Since the laws of kashrut are more elaborate than most dietary systems, the reader who is seeing this body of regulations for the first time may be slightly overwhelmed. The system is not as complex as it first appears, however. Once the basic principles are understood, the rest follows logically and naturally.

There are three fundamental areas to be concerned about: First, the animals and fishes that are permissible. Second, the use of meat and fowl: how it is to be slaughtered, where it can be bought, how it is to be prepared. Third, the separation of meat and dairy foods. The prohibition against mixing the two categories of food, explained below, extends not only to the foods eaten but also to the dishes and utensils used for cooking and eating.

The person who observes kashrut soon finds that it becomes second nature to plan meals, acquire kitchen equipment, do the grocery shopping, and manage the kitchen, bearing in mind the three basic principles: the separation of meat and dairy foods, permitted foods, and the preparation of meat.

Basic Definitions

Kosher (*kasher*, Hebrew)—Fit or proper for use.

Kashrut (Hebrew)—The system of Dietary Laws.

Treif (Yiddish) or *Trefah* (Hebrew)—The opposite of kosher, as applied to food; not suitable for use; forbidden. (The word literally means "torn by a wild beast." See, for example, Exodus 22:30.)

Meat (*fleishik*, Yiddish)—Any meat or poultry product or a product containing a meat derivative.

Dairy (*milkhik*, Yiddish)—Any milk or milk-based food.

Pareve (Yiddish)—Neither meat nor dairy; "neutral"; all fish; eggs, fruits, vegetables, and grains.

Separation of Meat and Dairy Foods

The law against mixing meat and dairy foods originates in the Bible, which notes in three places: "You shall not boil a kid in its mother's milk."[1] (See pages 44 and 101 for a discussion of the meaning of this law.)

The rabbis of the Talmud interpreted the verse to mean that no animal or animal product should come in contact with milk or a milk product. From this basic principle the following rules are derived:

Foods

1. Meat and milk products may not be eaten together at the same meal. They may not be cooked together or served as separate foods at one meal.

The rule includes baked goods and other prepared or processed foods. Bread, cake, cookies, and other desserts to be eaten at a meat meal should not contain milk, butter, or milk derivatives such as casein. (See Appendix, p. 96, "Additives.")

2. Pareve or "neutral" foods—fish, eggs, fruits, vegetables, and grains—may be eaten at both dairy and meat meals. Pareve foods cooked by themselves in a pot used for meat may be served at a dairy meal, and pareve foods cooked by themselves in a pot used for dairy may be served at a meat meal.

3. Artificial dairy products should be examined care-

fully. Margarine, creamers, dessert toppings and the like *may* contain milk or milk derivatives.

4.   Dairy and meat foods should not be cooked in a closed oven at the same time. Separate meat and dairy dishes may be cooked on top of the stove at the same time, so long as the pots are covered.

5.   Dairy products may not be eaten immediately after eating meat. The length of time one waits after eating meat before eating dairy products is a matter of custom: Among Jews from Western Europe, three hours; Jews from Eastern Europe, six hours; Jews from Holland, 72 minutes. In general, authorities recommend that we follow "the tradition of our ancestors." If this is not possible, the individual should establish his or her own tradition, keeping in mind the practice of the community in which he or she lives.[2]

6.   Meat may be eaten right after eating dairy foods (except hard cheeses), but it is desirable to create a break or to differentiate in some way, for example, by changing the tablecloth.

Utensils

The principle of separation between meat and dairy is observed by keeping separate dishes, pots and utensils for each category. The exact requirements are discussed in the next section, "The Kosher Kitchen."

The Kosher Kitchen

Basic Requirements

The basic requirements for having a kosher kitchen are twofold: there should be nothing nonkosher in it, and it should provide for separation of meat and dairy foods and utensils.

If it has been a *treif* or nonkosher kitchen, all traces of nonkosher food must be removed. Then, following a thorough cleaning, everything possible must go through the process known as "kashering."

Making Things Kosher

The process of kashering is used for three different purposes: converting a kitchen from nonkosher to kosher, preparing a kitchen for Passover, and "purifying" a utensil that has accidentally become nonkosher.

The two basic methods of kashering are (1) immersion in boiling water, or purging, and (2) exposure to open flame.

What Can Be Kashered

- Ranges and ovens;
- Refrigerators and freezers;
- Sinks;
- Dishwashers;
- Counters and tabletops;
- Most metal cooking utensils: pots, pans, flatware, and other kitchen ware;
- Utensils with a Teflon or other nonstick surface;
- Wooden bowls, unless they would be damaged by the heat of the kashering process;
- Plastics with high heat tolerance;
- Glassware;
- Ovenproof ceramics such as Pyrex, Corningware, and Corelle;
- Many small appliances (mixer, can opener, blender, processor, etc.). The criterion is whether the parts that come in contact with food, such as the beaters, blades, and contain-

ers, can be immersed in boiling water. If they cannot, the appliance cannot be kashered.

The exact steps to be followed in kashering are found in the Appendix (page 93).

What Cannot Be Kashered

- Melmac or other plastics that would melt if exposed to the required heat;
- Knives or other implements with wooden handles (food particles that lodge between the handle and the blade cannot be effectively removed by purging);
- Earthenware and other unglazed pottery (the material is absorbent and thus cannot be purged);
- Porcelain or other glazed pottery (China and fine porcelain which have not been used for twelve months are considered as new[3]).

Separating Meat and Dairy

The principle of separating between meat and dairy applies to all utensils used in the preparation and consumption of food. This is necessary because various materials absorb the flavor of food. If meat is cooked in a pot used for milk, for example, it is considered the same as mixing the two kinds of food, which is forbidden.

In practical terms, this means that a kosher home has to have at least two sets of dishes, flatware, pots, pans, and cooking implements. As a general rule, whatever is used for meat may not be used for dairy and vice versa. It is also desirable to store meat and dairy utensils in separate areas. (Since different dishes, etc., must be used during Passover, additional equipment is needed for that purpose. However, to ease the burden somewhat, flatware and certain other items used during the year can be kashered. See the section on Passover for details.)

Glassware: Most authorities hold that glass is not absorbent and that it does not retain the taste of food with which it comes in contact. Technically, therefore, one set of glass dishes could be used for meat and dairy.[4] This practice is discouraged, however, on at least two grounds. One, the use of the same dishes for everything could lead to carelessness and mixing of other utensils. Second, while glass might satisfy the letter of the law, the spirit of the law calls for making a clear distinction between the two categories of food.

Many people follow the practice of using the same glassware only for cold beverages and foods, such as salads and desserts.

Heatproof ceramics, such as Pyrex and Corningware, are considered the same as glass.[5]

Correcting a Mistake: If a pot, dish, or other utensil has accidentally been used for the wrong category, it must be kashered.

Dishwashing

- Meat and dairy utensils should not be washed together (a double sink comes in handy for this purpose);
- Separate sink racks and dish drainers should be used for each category;
- Separate dish towels, dish cloths and scouring pads should be used and clearly identified (usually by using different colors) for meat and dairy;
- Soaps and dishwashing detergents used should be produced with rabbinic supervision.

Using the Dishwasher

A dishwasher may be used for both dairy and meat dishes under the following conditions:

- Dairy and meat dishes should not be washed together;
- Dishes should be rinsed before being loaded into the dishwasher;
- The machine should be run through a rinse cycle between meat and dairy loads.[6]

Permitted Foods

1. All fresh *fruits and vegetables* are kosher. Canned and frozen foods and vegetables are usually permissible since manufacturers add only water and spices during the packaging process. Sometimes, however, fruits or vegetables are prepared with milk products or with nonkosher ingredients such as nonkosher meat broth. A careful reading of the ingredients is always necessary.[7]

2. All unprocessed grains and cereals are kosher. It is important to check the ingredients of processed items such as dry cereals or baked goods to make sure they have only kosher ingredients and, if desired, are free of dairy ingredients.[8]

3. All *milk and dairy products*, including cheese, are kosher and do not require rabbinical supervision.

This was not always the case. In ancient days, it was possible to adulterate milk with animal fats. Milk also might have come from nonkosher animals. Thus, it was customary to use only dairy products produced under rabbinical supervision. Under modern conditions, however, including government inspection, most authorities agree that there is no longer need for such supervision.

The status of cheese was the subject of controversy beginning in ancient times, and even today some people eat only cheese that has been rabbinically certified. The point at issue: Is rennet, a substance derived from an animal and used in cheesemaking, actually a meat product or even a food? Conservative authorities, and others, on the basis of extensive study of the subject, have concluded that rennet is not a food product, and thus no rabbinic supervision is needed.[9] (For additional information, see Appendix, p. 96, "Additives.")

4. *Eggs* from kosher fowl are kosher (and pareve). However, because of the prohibition against eating blood, an egg that contains a speck of blood may not be used. Eggs found inside a slaughtered chicken, with or without a shell covering, are considered as the chicken itself in terms of kashrut.[10]

5. All *fish* that have fins and scales are kosher. Excluded, as a group, are all shell fish. See Appendix, p. 82, for a listing of kosher and nonkosher fish commonly available in the United States.

6. *Meat:* The Torah explicitly defines the types of beasts and cattle considered kosher (Lev. 11:3 and Deut. 14:4). The main distinguishing signs are the cloven hoof and the fact that the animal chews its cud. Accordingly, the meat of cattle (beef and veal), sheep (lamb and mutton), and goats is permitted.[11] The meat of swine and rabbits is prohibited.

7. *Fowl:* Most domestic fowl are kosher, including the following: capon, duck (domestic), goose (domestic),[12] chicken, turkey, guinea fowl, house sparrow, palm dove, partridge, peacock, pheasant, pigeon, Cornish hen, quail, squab, and turtledove.[13]

Preparation of Meat

Buying Kosher Meat

The kosher butcher has a prime role in the observance of kashrut. The butcher is the one who purchases meat that is properly prepared, removes the forbidden parts of animals, and, in most instances, either automatically or upon request, will do the kashering (soaking and salting). It is important that the reliability of a kosher butcher be attested to by rabbinic authorities. The rabbi of a local congregation will usually provide the necessary information.

Several brands of frozen kosher meat and poultry products are now available in supermarkets and other outlets. The labels of these products should indicate that they have been supervised by competent rabbinic authorities.

Shechitah

Permitted animals and fowl must be slaughtered according to Jewish ritual requirements. (This does not apply to fish.) This should be done by a *shochet*, a ritual slaughterer, whose piety and knowledge of the laws of kashrut have been attested to by rabbinic authorities. Generally, *shochtim* are men, but we do have records of female ritual slaughterers.

The process of *shechitah* (ritual slaughter) is designed to cause the animal the least amount of pain, to bring about instant death, and to remove as much blood as possible. The method consists of cutting the throat with a single, swift, and uninterrupted horizontal sweep of the knife in such a way as to sever the trachea, esophagus, carotid arteries, and jugular vein. The knife blade must be perfect—sharper and smoother than a surgeon's scalpel and without the least perceptible nick.

The *shochet* then inspects the cut to make sure it has been made properly. The lungs of a mammal and the intestines of a fowl are among the organs that must be examined (*bedikah*) for various adhesions, discolorations, foreign objects, or other defects which make the animal unfit for kosher consumption.[14] The term *glatt* refers to a more stringent inspection procedure.[15]

Use of the Hindquarters

According to Genesis 32:32, it is forbidden to eat the sciatic nerve (*gid hanasheh*) of cattle and sheep (this does not apply to fowl). The custom commemorates the struggle of Jacob and the angel, and Jacob's injury. It is necessary, therefore, to remove the sciatic nerve, a procedure calling for special skill and training. Ashkenazic authorities have decided that we are not sufficiently expert in removing the *gid hanasheh*, and that kosher homes and restaurants may not serve meat from the hindquarters (containing T-bone and sirloin steaks).

In Sephardic communities, however, and in Israel, specially trained *menakrim* (people who remove veins and nerves) do exist, and it is possible to get kosher meat from the hindquarters.

Preparing Meat for Use (Kashering)

Since it is forbidden to eat the blood of an animal, the blood must be removed before the meat is cooked. This is done by a process called *kashering*, which involves either soaking and salting or broiling. It is usually possible to have the kosher butcher do the kashering, but one should not assume that the meat *is* kashered until this has been specifically determined. All frozen meat and poultry produced under rabbinical supervision have already been kashered.

Meat should be kashered within 72 hours of the slaughter of the animal. If an emergency makes it impossible to kasher the meat within that period, it should be thoroughly rinsed.

This rinsing begins a new 72-hour period and can be done up to three times. (When meat is shipped long distances, it is rinsed en route, under rabbinic supervision.)

Special Cases

Liver: Because it contains an excessive amount of blood, liver can *only* be kashered by broiling, and should not be soaked. (See below, "Broiling.") Even if liver is to be cooked some other way, it must first be broiled.

Ground meat: It is preferable that meat be kashered (that is, soaked and salted) before it is ground. It is then possible to prepare the chopped meat in any desired fashion. It is also best that the butcher have two machines, one for grinding unkashered meat and one for grinding kashered meat.

If the meat has not been kashered before grinding, the only permissible cooking method is broiling. (It is not possible to kasher meat after it is ground, since the salt will not reach all surfaces.) If chopped unkashered meat has been mixed with other ingredients, such as flour or eggs, it is not permitted even to broil the meat, since the added ingredients act as an obstruction to the blood flow.

Freezing: Meat should be kashered before it is frozen for subsequent use, unless it is going to be broiled. Since there are certain emergency situations when this rule can be relaxed, consult a rabbi if there are any questions.

Soaking and Salting

For kashering meat at home, the procedure is as follows:

1. The meat (this includes bones) is rinsed thoroughly with water.[16]

2. The meat is then soaked for half an hour in a vessel which is used only for this purpose. The water should

cover all the meat. (In an emergency, a shorter period of time is permissible.)

3. After the meat has soaked for half an hour, it is removed from the water and placed on a smooth, grooved incline or on a perforated surface, such as a rack. This is done so that the blood can drain off.

4. Coarse salt is spread on the meat, covering all sides so that no spot remains without salt. Poultry must be opened before salting in order that both the inside and outside are covered.

5. The salt that is used should be medium-coarse. Most markets carry "kosher salt" that is appropriate for kashering. (Fine salt melts too quickly and thus cannot purge the blood. Salt that is too coarse rolls off the meat.)

6. Poultry is placed on the salting board with the inside part downward so that the blood will not accumulate on the inside.

7. All inside parts of the fowl are removed before salting and are salted separately.

8. The gizzard is cut open and cleaned before kashering.

9. The meat remains in salt for about an hour. (In an emergency, a shorter period of time is permissible.)

10. After the meat is salted, it is rinsed thoroughly three times in clear, cold water.

11. For persons on a salt-restricted diet, only the minimum amount of salt should be used, for a minimum amount of time. The meat should then be boiled in a generous amount of liquid, and the broth thrown away (see Dr. Bruno Kisch, *Journal of the American Medical Association*, December 19, 1953). If a physician deter-

mines that the residual sodium even in this instance is excessive, ammonium chloride or potassium chloride may be used for the kashering process.

Broiling

Because broiling is considered the most effective procedure for the removal of blood from meat, meat that is to be broiled need not be kashered by soaking and salting. The procedure for kashering by broiling is as follows:

1. A small amount of salt (any salt will do) is sprinkled on the meat immediately before broiling.

2. The meat is placed on a grid or rack that lets the blood drip freely during the broiling process. The pan that catches the drippings should be used for no other purpose. Obviously, the blood dripping is considered *treif*.

3. The meat is broiled long enough so that there is a change of color and a crust is formed.

4. The meat is then turned, and the other side is salted and broiled.

Broilers

Meat may be broiled in an electric or gas broiler, or over an open fire, as on a barbecue.[17] It is essential that the blood be allowed to drip freely.

Processed Foods

Determining Whether a Product is Kosher

The wide variety of ingredients used in processed foods often makes it difficult to tell whether a product is kosher. Kosher consumers are helped by the growing use of rabbinical supervision by food producers, since a product that has been prepared under rabbinical supervision carries a symbol signifying that it is kosher. A list of acceptable kosher symbols is found on pages 72-73.

Kosher consumers are also helped by full disclosure of ingredients of products. However, the burden is on the consumer to examine listings of ingredients carefully and to learn something about the ingredients and additives that are used.

A product that does *not* have a kosher symbol can be judged by the following criteria:

If it contains any meat or meat derivative, it is not kosher.

Crackers, cookies, and other baked goods must be made with vegetable shortening *only*. If the package reads "shortening," that usually indicates the presence of at least some animal fats.

Food items that are to be used at meat meals should be checked to make sure that they do not contain milk products. Some commonly used "dairy" additives are casein, sodium caseinate, and lactose. (See Appendix for a list of kosher and pareve additives.)

Gelatin and Other Additives

Chemical additives present special problems and have received intensive study by rabbinic authorities working in conjunction with food chemists. Some substances that originate in animal sources undergo such complete change as a result of chemical treatment that they can no longer be regarded as "meat" products. This is the case with both gelatin and rennet, which Conservative authorities have ruled are kosher.

The Appendix provides an explanation of the legal principles involved as well as a listing of kosher and pareve additives.

Kosher Symbols

The common symbols in use in the United States and Canada today are listed below. If there is any question about the reliability of the supervision, a local congregational rabbi should be consulted.

Joint Kashruth Commission
Union of Orthodox Jewish Congregations of
America
116 East 27th St.
New York, NY 10016
212-725-3415

Kosher Supervision Service
733 Winthrop Road
Teaneck, NJ 07666
201-342-7400

Organized Kashruth Laboratories
P.O. Box 218
Brooklyn, NY 11204

Vaad Harabonim
177 Tremont St.
Boston, MA 02111
617-426-2139

K₀ Ko Kosher Service
5871 Drexel Road
Philadelphia, PA 19131
215-879-1100

Kosher Overseers Association of America
P.O. Box 1321
Beverly Hills, CA 90213
213-870-0011

COR   Council of Orthodox Rabbis

MK   Vaad Ha'ir of Montreal

K   The letter "K" is used on many packages and labels to note Kosher supervision. Since it cannot be copyrighted, anyone with rabbinical background may use it. Therefore, the kashrut of any product using this symbol should be investigated further.

The word "pareve" is used when no milk or meat products or derivatives are used. The letter "P" (such as KP, OP) means that the product is permissible for Passover use. The letter "M" (such as KM) is used when the product is considered dairy (*milkhik*) by the rabbinical authority.

Wine

All wines are kosher and thus do not require rabbinic certification.[18] (Brandy, cognac, sherry, vermouth, and champagne are wines.) During Passover, however, only wine that is certified kosher should be used.

Especially when wine is required for the fulfillment of a mitzvah, such as the ceremonies of circumcision, weddings, kiddush and havdalah, it is proper that the wine be certified kosher. To demonstrate support for the State of Israel, practically as well as symbolically, it is further recommended that Israeli wines (all of which are certified kosher) be used on all occasions.

It is of interest to know why, historically, only wine made under rabbinical supervision was permitted. The objection, in essence, was to using wine made by non-Jews. In ancient times, it was feared that the wine might be the same as that used for libations in idol worship (*yayin nesekh*), and all contact with idol worship was forbidden. In later periods, when idol worship had ceased, the prohibition against using wine made by non-Jews (*yeinam stam*) was seen as a means of limiting social contacts that might lead to intermarriage or to apostasy.

Passover

The distinctive aspect of this great festival, from the dietary standpoint, is the ban on eating any leavened food, or *chametz*. This prohibition is based on Exodus 12:15, in which the Bible commands: "Seven days you shall eat unleavened bread; on the very first day you shall remove leaven from your houses..."

Definition of Chametz

The Rabbis specified the five grains which become *chametz* as wheat, barley, spelt, rye, and oats. Ashkenazic authorities added to the list *kitniyot* and rice. *Kitniyot* are usually defined as beans, peas, lentils, corn, maize, millet, mustard, and other legumes. This prohibition applies to the *kitniyot* themselves, not to the oils or other liquids derived from them. Sephardic authorities prohibit only the original five grains and allow the use of legumes and rice during Passover.

Matzah may be made only from the five grains, but traditionally it has been made from wheat. Matzah must be completely baked within eighteen minutes after the water touches the flour. This process makes it possible to produce the matzah before there is any leavening.

General Laws

During Passover, it is forbidden not only to eat *chametz* but also to derive any benefit whatsoever from its use. This means that one may not run a business involved in the buying or selling of *chametz*, feed pets or animals with *chametz*, or even own *chametz*. All *chametz* must be completely removed from one's possession.

Removal of Chametz

In order to divest oneself of all *chametz*, several procedures are followed. First, all areas of the house are thoroughly cleaned and searched for *chametz*. (A person who rents a room from a non-Jew, e.g., a student living in a dormitory, is responsible only for the space he or she occupies.) The evening before the start of the holiday, a special search is held. This is called *bedikat chametz*. The procedure for carrying out this ritual is described in many *Haggadot*. In the course of the ceremony, the person renounces all leaven that may still be in his possession because it escaped detection. The following morning, any remaining leaven that has been found is burned.

Sale of Chametz: Since it is sometimes impossible to destroy all the *chametz* in one's possession, a special sale called *mekhirat chametz* is arranged through a rabbi. The *chametz* is sold to a non-Jew, who becomes its legal owner for the week of Passover (the rabbi "repurchases" it after the holiday). Technically, therefore, the *chametz* is removed from the Jew's possession.

All material to be sold should be isolated from the food and utensils used on Passover. Pets and other animals should also be sold (although they remain in the house as usual), since most animal food contains *chametz*.

Preparing the Kitchen

All forbidden foods are removed (see list below). Every nook and cranny of the kitchen is scrubbed so as to make certain that all crumbs and other food residues are destroyed.

Dishes used during the year are put away and replaced by dishes reserved for Passover. Flatware, pots, and other utensils that can be kashered may be used (except for baking pans). Items that cannot be kashered should be replaced with items used only for Passover. (See "The Kosher Kitchen" and Appendix, p. 93, for details about what can be kashered and the procedures to follow.)

Appliances and sinks are cleaned and kashered. Stove and refrigerator shelves, drip trays, counters and other surfaces that can be covered are covered with aluminum foil or other suitable materials.

The kashering and preparation of the kitchen should be completed by 9:00 A.M. on the 14th of Nisan, the day of the first Seder.

Food

Any food that contains *chametz* or that has come in contact with *chametz* during preparation is forbidden. That is why special care must be taken with Passover foods. While the law provides several remedies if a mistake is made during food preparation throughout the rest of the year, these remedies do not apply to *chametz*.

Forbidden Foods: Leavened bread, cakes, biscuits, crackers, cereals, coffee substances mixed with grain, anything made from the five forbidden grains (with the exception of matzah and other products made under rabbinical supervision), or anything made from the forbidden sources, such as beer and liquor (with the exception of products made under rabbinical supervision).

The designation *"Kosher L'Pesach"* applied to a food product means that it has been prepared under rabbinic supervision to assure that no *chametz* was used in its preparation and that only proper utensils were used. Care should be taken to note that the words "*Kosher L'Pesach*" be on a non-detachable label, preferably with the name of the rabbi who has supervised preparation of the product.

Foods Requiring No "Kosher L'Pesach" Label: The following foods in *unopened* packages or containers: pure coffee, pure tea, milk, sugar (except for powdered/confectioner's), honey, dried fruits, nuts (except legumes), salt, pepper, onion powder, garlic powder, and any other spice that is permitted on Passover, fresh fruits and vegetables (except legumes and corn). All fruits and vegetables should be washed thoroughly before use.

Fruits and vegetables which are permitted in their natural state are permitted in their frozen state.

Medicines: Because the principle of *pikuach nefesh* (the preservation of life) takes precedence over all other laws, medicines prescribed by a doctor in connection with life-sustaining therapy are permitted on Passover. Other substances used for medical purposes (e.g., aspirin, vitamins, tranquilizers), while perhaps not made from *chametz*, may contain *chametz* used as a binder. In most instances, a pharmacist should be able to supply the information needed regarding the origins and sources of drugs.[19]

Cosmetics: Most toothpastes, lotions, ointments, and creams are permissible. However, cosmetics made from a grain alcohol base are regarded as *chametz*.

Baby Food: Baby food for Passover is available in many places. If it is absolutely necessary to use ordinary baby food, it should be prepared in a separate part of the house where it does not come in contact with the family food.

Pet Food: Most pet foods contain *chametz*, and it is forbidden to benefit from *chametz* on Passover. If an owner feeds his pet *chametz* which is in his possession, he is deriving benefit from it. Therefore, rabbinic authorities advise that pets and pet food be included in the sale of *chametz*. Thus, in a technical legal framework, the non-Jewish, temporary owner (and not the Jewish owner) will be benefitting when the pet is fed. Care should be taken that the *chametz* pet food be clearly separated from other foods and that the pet not drag bits of the pet food into other parts of the home.

Eating Out

Owing to the small number of kosher facilities available in the United States and Canada, situations frequently arise which make it necessary to relax the strict standards of kashrut observed in the home. When one is in such a predicament, the following principles should apply:

1. A thorough investigation should be made to ascertain whether there are kosher facilities available within a reasonable distance.[20] These facilities might be found in vegetarian or dairy restaurants. Preference should always be given to kosher facilities even when nonkosher facilities are more appealing.

2. If it is necessary to dine in nonkosher facilities, meat and dishes containing meat may not be eaten. Some kashrut observers sanction the eating of cold foods, such as salads, if the food contains no forbidden ingredients. Still others approve eating permitted fish and other foods, even if cooked.

3. Functions sponsored by Jewish organizations, such as synagogue groups and national Jewish organizations, should be strictly kosher, with the food prepared under

rabbinic supervision. Furthermore, *se'udot shel mitzvah* (e.g., weddings, bar mitzvahs, and *brit* ceremonies) should be kosher.

4. A student choosing a college is advised to inquire about the availability of kosher food, or facilities for doing one's own cooking.[21]

5. All national and international airlines will provide kosher or vegetarian meals if requested ahead of time. This is also true of many hospitals, hotels and resorts.

6. Jews wishing to observe the dietary laws in the Armed Services should see their chaplain.

Other Traditions Regarding Eating

The Jewish home is sanctified by the observance of kashrut. In addition to the regulations concerning food, the table itself is regarded as an altar of holiness. In order to realize this goal, Jewish tradition has prescribed the following:

1. *Ritual Washing of the Hands:* Washing the hands is not only a hygienic measure, it is also a religious ceremony. Therefore a special blessing has been ordained to be recited immediately before drying the hands. The water should be poured on the hands from a glass or some other vessel. The blessing is:

Barukh atah Adonai, Eloheinu Melekh ha-olam, asher kid'shanu b'mitzvotav, v'tzivanu al n'tilat yadayim.

Praised are You, Lord our God, King of the universe who has sanctified us through His commandments and commanded us concerning the washing of the hands.

2.   *The Blessing Over the Bread:* Immediately after washing the hands (without any interruption, even of talking), a blessing should be pronounced over the bread:

Barukh atah Adonai, Eloheinu Melekh ha-olam, ha-motzi lechem min haaretz.

Praised are You, Lord our God, King of the universe who brings forth bread from the earth.

If one pronounces this blessing it is not ordinarily necessary to pronounce any other blessing during the meal. It is customary to sprinkle salt on the bread before it is eaten.

3.   *Grace After Meals:*

a. After the meal, Grace is recited.

b. Prior to the recitation of the Grace, it is customary to cover or remove any knives which happen to be on the table. Since knives are considered symbols of violence, they disrupt the symbolism of the table as an altar when they serve no function (as they do during the meal).

Cooking on Shabbat

Both the tending of fire and cooking are among the Biblical prohibitions against work on Shabbat. A distinction was made, however, between cooking and warming. The following conditions should be observed:

1.   It is permissible only to reheat previously cooked foods.

2.   The flame or electric heat should not be adjusted. If a burner is left on during Shabbat, it should be covered with a *blech* (tin plate), to prevent the possibility of inadvertently adjusting the stove or oven.

3. Solids, no matter what temperature, may be warmed.

4. Liquids may be warmed as long as the fire is not hot enough to bring them to a boil.[22]

Taking Challah

It is customary during the baking of bread to remove a small portion of the kneaded dough to commemorate the tithe given to the priests during the time of the Temple. The piece taken is usually the size of an olive, and it is burned in the oven at the same time as the bread bakes.[23] Dough not burned in the oven is thrown away. The custom is generally that "*challah*" should be taken in any recipe using at least three pounds of flour. If three or more pounds of flour are used, the following blessing is said:

Barukh atah Adonai, Eloheinu Melekh ha-olam, asher kid'shanu b'mitzvotav, v'tzivanu l'haphrish challah.

Praised are You, Lord our God, King of the universe who has sanctified us through His commandments and commanded us to separate *challah*.

It is doubtful whether *challah* must be taken if eggs or fruit juice are used in the dough.

APPENDIX

Kosher and Nonkosher Fishes

Kosher Fishes

Albacore, *see* Mackerels

Alewife, *see* Herrings

Amberjack, *see* Jacks

Anchovies (Family Engraulidae), including European anchovy (Engraulis encrasicolus); Northern or California anchovy (Engraulis mordax)

Angelfishes and butterfly fishes (Family Chaetodontidae), including Angelfishes (Holacanthus species, Pomacanthus species)

Angler, *see* Goosefishes (nonkosher)

Atlantic Pomfret or Ray's bream (Brama brama)

Ballyhoo, *see* Flyingfishes

Barracudas (Family Sphyracnidae), including Barracudas and kakus (Sphyraena species)

Bass, *see* Sea basses; Temperate basses; Sunfishes; Drums

Beluga; *see* Sturgeons

Bigeyes (Family Priancanthidae), including Bigeyes or aweoweos (Priacanthus species)

Blackfish, *see* Carps; Wrasses

Blacksmith, *see* Damselfishes

Blowfish, *see* Puffers (nonkosher)

Blueback, *see* Flounders; Herrings; Trouts

Bluefish or snapper blue (Pomatomus saltatrix)

Bluegill, *see* Sunfishes

Bocaccio, *see* Scorpionfishes

Bombay duck (Harpadon nehereus)

Bonefish (Albula vulpes)

Bonito, *see* Cobia; Mackerels

Bowfin, freshwater dogfish, or grindle (Amia calva)

Bream, *see* Carps; Atlantic pomfret; Porgies

Brill, *see* Flounders

Buffalo fishes, *see* Suckers

Bullhead, *see* Catfishes (nonkosher)

Burbot, *see* Codfishes

Butterfishes (Family Stromateidae), including Butterfish (Peprilus triacanthus); Pacific pompano (Peprilus simillimus); Harvestfishes (Peprilus species)

Butterfly fish, *see* Angelfish

Cabezon, *see* Sculpins (nonkosher)

Cabrilla, *see* Sea basses

Calico bass, *see* Sunfishes

Capelin, *see* Smelts

Carps and minnows (Family Cyprinidae), including the carp, leather carp, mirror carp (Cyprinus carpio); Crucian carp (Carassius carassius); Goldfish (Carassius auratus); Tench (Tinca tinca); Splittail (Pogonichthys macrolepidotus); Squawfishes (Ptychocheilus species); Sacramento blackfish or hardhead (Orthodon microlepidotus); Freshwater breams (Abramis species, Blicca species); Roach (Rutilus rutilus)

Carpsuckers, *see* Suckers

°Caviar, from Trouts and whitefishes (salmon), kosher Sturgeons. Lumpsuckers (nonkosher)

Cero, *see* Mackerels

Channel bass, *see* Drums

Char, *see* Trouts

Chilipepper, *see* Scorpionfishes

Chinook salmon, *see* Trouts

Chub, *see* Trouts; Sea chubs

Cichlids (Family Cichlidae), including Tilapias (Tilapia species); Mozambique mouthbrooder (Tilapia mossambica); Cichlids (Cichlasoma species); Rio Grande perch (Cichlasoma cyanoguttatum)

Cigarfish, *see* Jacks

Cisco, *see* Trouts

Coalfish, *see* Codfishes

Cobia, cabio, or black bonito (Rachycentron canadum)

Cod, cultus, black, blue, or ling, *see* Greenlings; Sablefish

Codfishes (Family Gadidae), including Cod (Gadus morhua); Haddock (Melanogrammus aeglefinus); Pacific cod (Gadus macrocephalus); Pollock, saithe, or coalfish (Pollachius virens); Walleye pollock (Theragra chalcogramma); Hakes (Urophycis species); Whiting (Meriangius merlangus); Blue whiting or poutassou (Micromesistius poutassou); Burbot, lawyer, or freshwater ling (Lota lota); Tomcods or frostfishes (Microgradus species)

Coho salmon, *see* Trouts

Corbina or corvina, *see* Drums

Cottonwick, *see* Grunts

Crappie, *see* Sunfishes

Crevalle, *see* Jacks

Croaker, *see* Drums

°Caviar is the roe or eggs from various varieties of fish. If the fish from which the caviar is made is kosher, then the resultant caviar is kosher.

Crucian carp, *see* Carps
Cubbyu, *see* Drums
Cunner, *see* Wrasses

Dab, *see* Flounders
Damselfishes (Family Pomacentridae), including Blacksmith (Chromis punctipinnis); Garibaldi (Hypsypops rubicunda)
Doctorfish, *see* Sturgeonfishes
Dogfish, *see* Bowfin, Sharks (nonkosher)
Dolly Varden, *see* Trouts
°Dolphin fishes or mahimahis (Coryphaena species)
Drums and croakers (Family Sciaenidae), including Seatrouts and corvinas (Cynoscion species); Weakfish (Cynoscion nebulosus); White seabass (Cynoscion nobilis); Croakers (Micropogon species, Bairdiella species, Odontoscion species); Silver perch (Bairdiella chrysura); White or king croaker (Genyonemus lineatus); Black croaker (Cheilotrema saturnum); Spotfin croaker (Roncador stearnsi); Yellowfin croaker (Umbrina roncador); Drums (Pogonias species, Stellifer species, Umbrina species); Red drum or channel bass (Sciaenops ocellata); Freshwater drum (Aplodinotus grunniens); Kingfishes or king whitings (Menticirrhus species); California corbina (Menticirrhus undulatus); Spot or lafayette (Leiostomus xanthurus); Queenfish (Seriphus politus); Cubbyu or ribbon fish (Equetus umbrosus)

Eulachon, *see* Smelts

Flounders (Families Bothidae and Pleuronectidae), including Flounders (Paralichthys species, Liopsetta species, Platichthys species, etc.); Starry flounder (Platichthys stellatus); Summer flounder or fluke (Paralichthys dentatus); Yellowtail flounder (Limanda ferrugina); Winter flounder, lemon sole, or blackback (Pseudopleuronectes americanus); Halibut (Hippoglossus species); California halibut (Paralichthys californicus); Bigmouth sole (Hippoglossina stomata); Butter or scalyfin sole (Isopsetta isolepis); "Dover" sole (Microstomus pacificus); "English" sole (Parophrys vetulus); Fantail sole (Xystreurys liolepis); Petrale sole (Eopsetta jordani); Rex sole (Glyptocephalus zachirus);

°Not to be confused with the Mammal called Dolphin or Porpoise, which is nonkosher.

Rock sole (Lepidopsetta bilineata); Sand sole (Psettichthys melanostictus); Slender sole (Lyopsetta exilis); Yellowfin sole (Limanda aspera); Pacific turbots (Pleuronichthys species); Curlfin turbot or sole (Pleuronichthys decurrens); Diamond turbot (Hypsopsetta guttulata); Greenland turbot or halibut (Reinhardtius hippoglossoides); Sanddabs (Citharichthys species); Dabs (Limanda species); American plaice (Hippoglossoides platessoides); European plaice (Pleuronectes platessa); Brill (Scophthalmus rhombus); but not including European turbot (Scophthalmus maxima or Psetta maximus)

Fluke, *see* Flounders

Flyingfishes and halfbeaks (Family Exocoetidae); Flyingfishes (Cypselurus species and others); Ballyhoo or balao (Hemiramphus species)

Frostfish, *see* Codfishes

Gag, *see* Sea basses

Gar, *see* Needlefishes; Gars (nonkosher)

Garibaldi, *see* Damselfishes

Giant kelpfish (Heterostichus rostratus)

Gizzard shad, *see* Herrings

Goatfishes or surmullets (Family Mullidae), including Goatfishes (Mullus species, Pseudupeneus species); Wekes or goatfishes (Mulloidichthys species, Upeneus species); Kumu (Parupeneus species); Red mullet (Mullus surmuletus)

Gobies (Family Gobiidae), including Bigmouth sleeper or guavina (Gobiomorus dormitor); Sirajo goby (Sicydium plumieri)

Goldeye and mooneye (Hiodon alosoides and Hiodon tergisus)

Goldfish, *see* Carps

Grayfish, *see* Sharks (nonkosher)

Grayling, *see* Trouts

Graysby, *see* Sea basses

Greenlings (Family Hexagrammidae), including Greenlings (Hexagrammos species); Kelp greenling or seatrout (Hexagrammos decagrammus); Lingcod, cultus or blue cod (Ophiodon elongatus); Atka mackerel (Pleurogrammus monopteryglus)

Grindle, *see* Bowfin

Grouper, *see* Sea basses

Grunion, *see* Silversides

Grunts (Family Pomadasyidae), including Grunts (Haemulon species, Pomadasys species); Margate (Haemulon album); Tomtate (Haemulon aurolineatum); Cottonwick (Haemulon melanurum); Sailors choice (Haemulon parrai); Porkfish (Anisotremus virginicus); Black margate (Anisotremus surinamensis); Sargo

(Anisotremus davidsoni); Pig-fish (Orthopristis chrysop-tera)

Guavina, *see* Gobies

Haddock, *see* Codfishes

Hake, *see also* Codfishes

Hakes (Family Merlucciidae), including Hakes (Merluccius species); Silver hake or whit-ing (Merluccius bilinearis); Pacific hake or merluccio (Merluccius productus)

Halfbeak, *see* Flyingfishes

Halfmoon, *see* Sea chubs

Halibut, *see* Flounders

Hamlet, *see* Sea basses

Hardhead, *see* Carps

Harvestfish, *see* Butterfishes

Hawkfishes (Family Cirrhiti-dae), including Hawkfishes (Cirrhitus species)

Herrings (Family Clupeidae), including Atlantic and Pacific herring (Clupea harengus subspecies); Thread herrings (Opisthonema species); Shads (Alosa species); Shad or glut herring, or blueback (Alosa aestivalis); Hickory shad (Alosa mediocris); Alewife or river herring (Alosa pseudo-harengus); Gizzard shads (Dorosoma species); Menha-dens or mossbunkers (Bre-voortia species); Spanish sar-dine (Sardinella anchovia); European sardine or pilchard (Sardina pilchardus); Pacific sardine or pilchard (Sardi-nops sagax); Sprat (Sprattus sprattus)

Hind, *see* Sea basses

Hogchoker, *see* Soles

Hogfish, *see* Wrasses

Horse mackerel, *see* Jacks

Jack mackerel, *see also* Jacks

Jacks and pompanos (Family Carangidae), including Pom-panos, palometas, and per-mits (Trachinotus species); Amberjacks and yellowtails (Seriola species); California yellowtail (Seriola dorsalis); Scads and cigarfish (Decap-terus species, Selar species, Trachurus species); Jack mackerel or horse mackerel (Trachurus symmetricus); Jacks and uluas (Caranx spe-cies, Carangoldes species); Crevalles (Caranx species); Blue runner (Caranx crysos); Rainbow runner (Elagatis bi-pinnulata); Moonfishes (Vo-mer species); Lookdown (Se-lene vomer); Leatherback or lae (Scomberoides sanctipe-tri); but not including Leath-erjacket (Oligoplites saurus)

Jacksmelt, *see* Silversides

Jewfish, *see* Sea basses

John Dory (Zeus faber)

Kelpfish, *see* Giant kelpfish

Kingfish, *see* Drums, Mackerels

Ladyfish, or tenpounder (Elops saurus)

Lafayette, *see* Drums

Lake herring, *see* Trouts

Lance or launce, *see* Sand lances

Largemouth bass, *see* Sunfishes

Lawyer, *see* Codfishes

Leatherjacket, *see* Jacks

Leatherjacket, *see also* Jacks (nonkosher)

Lingcod, *see* Greenlings

Lizardfishes (Family Synodontidae)

Lookdown, *see* Jacks

Mackerel, *see also* Jacks

Mackerel, Atka, *see* Greenlings

Mackerels and tunas (Family Scombridae), including Mackerels (Scomber species, Scomberomorus species, Auxis species); Spanish mackerels, cero, and sierra (Scomberomorus species); King mackerel or kingfish (Scomberomorus cavalla); Bonitos (Sarda species); Wahoo Acanthocybium solanderi); Tunas (Thunnus species, Euthynnus species); Skipjack tunas (Euthynnus or Katsuwonus species); Albacore (Thunnus alalunga); but not including Snake mackerels

Mahimahi, *see* Dolphin fishes

Margate, *see* Grunts

Marlin, *see* Billfishes (nonkosher)

Menhaden, *see* Herrings

Menpachii, *see* Squirrelfishes

Merluccio, *see* Hakes

Midshipman, *see* Toadfishes (nonkosher)

Milkfish or awa (Chanos chanos)

Mojarras (Family Gerreidae), including Mojarras (Eucinostomus species, Gerres species, Diapterus species)

Monkeyface prickleback or eel (Cebidichthys violaceus)

Mooneye, *see* Goldeye

Moonfish, *see* Jacks

Mossbunker, *see* Herrings

Mouthbrooder, *see* Cichlids

Mullet, *see* Goatfishes

Mullets (Family Mugilidae), including Mullets and amaamas (Mugil species); Uouoa (Neomyxus chaptalii); Mountain mullets or dajaos (Agonostomus species)

Muskellunge, *see* Pikes

Mutton hamlet, *see* Sea basses

Muttonfish, *see* Snappers

Needlefishes (Family Belonidae); Needlefishes or marine gars (Strongylura species, Tylosurus species)

Opaleye, *see* Sea chubs

Paddlefish, *see* Sturgeons (kosher)

Palometa, *see* Jacks

Parrotfishes (Family Scaridae), including Parrotfishes and uhus (Scarus species, Sparisoma species)

Perch, *see also* Temperate

basses; Drums; Cichlids; Surfperches; Scorpionfishes

Perches (Family Percidae), including Yellow perch (Perca
flavescens); Walleye, pike-
perch, or yellow or blue pike
(Stizostedion vitreum); Sauger (Stizostedion canadense)

Permit, *see* Jacks

Pickerel, *see* Pike

Pigfish, *see* Grunts

Pike, *see* Perches

Pikes (Family Esocidae), including Pike (Esox lucius);
Pickerels (Esox species); Muskellunge (Esox masquinongy)

Pike-perch, *see* Perches

Pilchard, *see* Herrings

Pinfish, *see* Porgies

Plaice, *see* Flounders

Pollock, *see* Codfishes

Pomfret, *see* Atlantic pomfret

Pompano, *see* Jacks; Butterfishes

Porgies and sea breams (Family
Sparidae), including Porgies
(Calamus species, Diplodus
species, Pagrus species); Scup
(Stenotomus chrysops); Pin-
fish (Lagodon rhomboides);
Sheepshead (Archosargus
probatocephalus)

Porkfish, *see* Grunts

Pout, *see* Ocean pout (nonkosher)

Poutassou, *see* Codfishes

Prickleback, *see* Monkeyface
prickleback; Rockprickle-
back (nonkosher)

Queenfish, *see* Drums

Quillback, *see* Suckers

Rabalo, *see* Snooks

Ratfish, *see* Sharks (nonkosher)

Ray, *see* Sharks (nonkosher)

Ray's bream, *see* Atlantic pomfret

Red snapper, *see* Snappers

Redfish, *see* Scorpionfishes;
Wrasses

Roach, *see* Carps

Rock bass, *see* Sunfishes

Roch hind, *see* Sea basses

Rockfish, *see* Scorpionfishes;
Temperate basses

Rosefish, *see* Scorpionfishes

Rudderfish, *see* Sea chubs

Runner, *see* Jacks

Sablefish or black cod (Aneplo-
poma fimbria)

Sailfish, *see* Billfishes (nonkosher)

Sailors choice, *see* Grunts

Saithe, *see* Codfishes

Salmon, *see* Trouts

Sand lances, launces, or eels
(Ammodytes species)

Sardine, *see* Herrings

Sargo, *see* Grunts

Sauger, *see* Perches

Scad, *see* Jacks

Scamp, *see* Sea basses

Schoolmaster, *see* Snappers

Scorpionfishes (Family Scor-
paenidae), including Scorpionfishes (Scorpaena species);
California scorpionfish or
sculpin (Scorpaena guttata);
Nohus (Scorpaenopsis spe-
cies); Redfish, rosefish, or

ocean perch (Sebastes marinus); Rockfishes (Sebastes species, Sebastodes species); Pacific ocean perch (Sebastes alutus); Chilipepper (Sebastes goodei); Bocaccio (Sebastes paucispinus); Shortspine thornyhead or channel rockfish (Sebastolobus alascanus)

Scup, *see* Porgies

Sea bass, *see also* Temperate basses; Drums

Sea basses (Family Serranidae), including Black sea basses (Centropristis species); Groupers (Epinephelus species and Mycteroperca species); Rock hind (Epinephelus adscensionis); Speckled hind (Epinephelus drummondhayi); Red hind (Epinephelus guttatus); Jewfish (Epinephelus itajara); Spotted cabrilla (Epinephelus analogus); Gag (Mycteroperca microlepis); Scamp (Mycteroperca phenax); Graysby (Petrometopon cruentatum); Mutton hamlet (Alphestes afer); Sand bass, kelp bass, and spotted bass (Paralabrax species)

Sea bream, *see* Porgies

Sea chubs (Family Kyphosidae), including Bermuda chub or rudderfish (Kyphosus sectatrix); Opaleye (Girella nigricans); Halfmoon Medialuna californiensis)

Seaperch, *see* Surfperches

Searaven, *see* Sculpins (nonkosher)

Searobins (Family Triglidae); Searobins (Prionotus species)

Sea-squab, *see* Puffers (nonkosher)

Seatrout, *see* Drums; Greenlings; Steelhead

Shad, *see* Herrings

Sheepshead, *see* Porgies; Wrasses

Sierra, *see* Mackerels

Silversides (Family Atherinidae), including Whitebait, spearing, or silversides (Menidia species); California grunion (Leuresthes tenuis); Jacksmelt (Atherinopsis californiensis); Topsmelt (Atherinops affinis)

Sirajo goby, *see* Gobies

Skates, *see* Sharks (nonkosher)

Skipjack, *see* Mackerels

Sleeper, *see* Gobies

Smallmouth bass, *see* Sunfishes

Smelts (Family Osmeridae), including Smelts (Osmerus species); Capelin (Mallotus villosus); Eulachon (Taleichthys pacificus)

Snapper blue, *see* Bluefish

Snappers (Family Lutjanidae), including Snappers (Lutjanus species); Schoolmaster (Lutjanus apodus); Muttonfish or mutton snapper (Lutjanus analis); Red snapper (Lutjanus) campechanus); Yellowtail snapper (Ocyurus chrysurus); Kalikali (Pristipomoides sieboldi); Opakapaka (Pristipomoides microlepis); Onaga (Etelis carbunculus)

Snooks (Family Centropomidae), including Snooks or rabalos (Centropomus species)

Sockeye salmon, *see* Trouts

Sole, *see also* Flounders

Soles (Family Soleidae), including Sole or true sole (Solea solea); Lined sole (Achirus lineatus); Hogchoker (Trinecies maculatus)

Spadefishes (Family Ephippidae), including Spadefishes (Chaetodipterus species)

Spanish mackerel, *see* Mackerels

Spearing, *see* Silversides

Splittail, *see* Carps

Spoonbill cat, *see* Sturgeons (nonkosher)

Spot, *see* Drums

Sprat, *see* Herrings

Squawfish, *see* Carps

Squirrelfishes (Family Holocentridae), including Squirrelfishes (Holocentrus species); Menpachii (Myripristis species)

Steelhead, *see* Trouts

Striped bass, *see* Temperate basses

*Sturgeons (Order Acipenseriformes), including Sturgeons (Acipenser species, Scaphirhynchus species); Beluga (huso huso); Paddlefish or spoonbill cat (Polyodon spathula)

Suckers (Family Catostomidae), including Buffalo fishes (Ictiobus species); Suckers (Catostomus species, Moxostoma species); Quillbacks or carpsuckers (Carplodes species)

Sunfishes (Family Centrarchidae), including Freshwater basses (Micropterus species); Largemouth bass (Micropterus salmoides); Small mouth bass (Micropterus dolomieui); Sunfishes (Lepomis species); Bluegill (Lepomis macrochirus); Warmouth (Lepomis gulosus); Rock bass or red dye (Ambloplites rupestris); Crappies or calico basses (Pomoxis species)

Surfperches (Family Embiotocidae), including Surfperches (Amphistichus species, Hyperprosopon species); Seaperches (Embiotoca species, Hypsurus species, Phanerodon species, Rhacochilus species); Black perch (Embiotoca jacksoni); Pile perch (Rhacochilus vacca); Shiner perch (Cymatogaster aggregata)

Surgeonfishes (Family Acanthuridae), including Surgeonfishes and tangs (Acanthurus

---

*The kashrut of Sturgeon centers on the definition of sturgeon's shields as scales. This is discussed in *Hapardes* (Volume 7, Numbers 1 & 5, 1933).

species, Zebrasoma species);
Doctorfish (Acanthurus chirurgus); Unicornfishes or kalas (Naso species)

*Swordfish (Xiphias gladius)

Tang, see Surgeonfishes

Tarpon (Megalops atlantica)

Tautog, see Wrasses

Temperate basses (Family Percichthyidae), including Striped bass or rockfish (Morone saxatillis); Yellow bass (Morone mississippiensis); White bass (Morone chrysops); White perch (Morone americana); Giant California sea bass (Stereolepsis gigas)

Tench, see Carps

Tenpounder, see Ladyfish

Threadfins (Family Polynemidae), including Blue bobo (Polydactylus approximans); Barbu (Polydactylus virginicus); Moi (Polydactylus sexfilis)

Tilapia, see Cichlids

Tilefishes (Family Branchiostegidae), including Tilefish (Lopholatilus chamaeleonticeps); Ocean whitefish (Caulolatilus princeps)

Tomcod, see Codfishes

Tomtate, see Grunts

Topsmelt, see Silversides

Tripletail (Lobotes surinamensis)

Trouts and whitefishes (Family Salmonidae), including Atlantic salmon (Salmo salar); Pacific salmons (Oncorhynchus species), Coho or silver salmon, sockeye, blueback or red salmon, chinook, king or spring salmon, pink or humpback salmon, chum, dog, or fall salmon; Trouts (Salmo species), Brown trout, rainbow trout or steelhead, cutthroat trout, golden trout; Chars (Salvelinus species), Lake trout, brook trout, Arctic char, Dolly Varden; Whitefishes and ciscos (Coregonus species and Prosopium species); Cisco or lake herring (Coregonus artedii); Chubs (Coregonus species); Graylings (Thymallus species)

Tuna, see Mackerels

Turbot, see Flounders

Unicornfish, see Surgeonfishes

Wahoo, see Mackerels

Walleye, see Perches

Walleye pollock, see Codfishes

Warmouth, see Sunfishes

Weakfish, see Drums

---

*Swordfish is kosher according to Klein in *Proceedings* 1966. For contra see Tendler and the Union of Orthodox Jewish Congregations pub. *Kashruth: Handbook For Home and School.*

Whitebait, *see* Silversides

Whitefish, *see* Trouts; Tilefishes

Whiting, *see* Codfishes; Hakes; Drums

Wrasses (Family Labridae), including Hogfishes and aawas (Bodianus species); Hogfish or capitaine (Lachnolaimus maximus); Tautog or blackfish (Tautoga onitis); California sheephead or redfish (Pimelometopon pulchrum); Cunner, chogset, or bergall (Tautogolabrus adspersus)

Yellowtail, *see* Jacks

Yellowtail snapper, *see* Snappers

Nonkosher Fishes

Bullfishes (Family Istiophoridae), including Sailfishes (Istiophorus species); Marlins and spearfishes (Tetrapterus species, Makaira species)

Catfishes (Order Siluriformes), including Channel catfish (Ictalurus punctatus), Bullheads (Ictalurus species); Sea catfish (Arius felis)

Cutlassfishes (Family Trichiuridae), including Cutlassfishes (Trichiurus species); Scabbardfishes (Lepidopus species)

Eels (Order Anguilliformes), including American and European eel (Anguilla rostrata and Anguilla anguilla); Conger eel (Conger oceanicus)

Gars (Order Semionotiformes); Freshwater gars (Lepisosteus species)

Goosefishes or angles (Lophius species)

Lampreys (Family Petromyzontidae)

Leatherjacket (Oligoplites saurus)

Lumpsuckers (Family Cyclopteridae), including Lumpfish (Cyclopterus lumpus); Snailfishes (Liparis species)

Monkfish

Ocean pout or eelpout (Macrozoarces americanus)

Oilfish (Ruvettus pretiosus)

Puffers (Family Tetraodontidae); Puffers, blowfishes, swellfishes, sea-squab (Sphoeroides species)

Rock prickleback or rockeel (Xiphistae mucosus)

Sculpins (Family Cottidae),

including Sculpins (Myoxocephalus species, Cottus species, Leptocottus species, etc.); Cabezon (Scorpaenichthys marmoratus); Searaven (Hemitripterus americanus)

Sharks, rays and their relatives (Class Chondrichthyes), including Grayfishes or dogfishes (Mustelus species, Squalus species); Souptin shark (Galeothinus zyopterus); Sawfishes (Pristis species); Skates (Raja species); Chimaeras or ratfishes (Order Chimaeriformes)

Snake mackerels (Gempylus species)

Toadfishes (Family Batrachoididae), including Toadfishes (Opsanus species); Midshipmen (Porichthys species)

Triggerfishes and filefishes (Family Balistidae); Triggerfishes (Balistes species, Canthidermis species)

Trunkfishes (Family Ostraciidae); Trunkfishes and cowfishes (Lactophrys species)

Wolffishes (Family Anarchichadidae), including Wolffishes or ocean catfishes (Anarchichas species)

This list of fishes has been adapted from a list prepared by Dr. James W. Atz, Curator and Dean Bibliographer in the Department of Ichthyology of The American Museum of Natural History in New York City.

Kashering Utensils, Appliances, and Surfaces

The process of kashering is used in three cases: (1) converting a nonkosher kitchen to a kosher kitchen; (2) making a kitchen kosher for Passover; (3) correcting a mistake which rendered a utensil nonkosher.

Kashering Utensils

There are two basic methods of kashering utensils.

Purging: Most cooking utensils can be made kosher by immersion in boiling water. This includes metal pots, most pans including nonstick pans, flatware, plastic with high heat tolerance, and many other kinds of kitchen ware. The procedure is as follows:

1. The article to be kashered is thoroughly scoured.

2. The article is set aside and not used for 24 hours.

3. The article is completely immersed in a pot of boiling (rolling boil) water.

4. If a pot is too large to fit into another pot, the pot to be kashered is filled to the brim with water, and that water is brought to a boil. While the water is still boiling, a hot stone or piece of metal is dropped into the pot in order that the water remain at its peak heat and also that it boil over the side of the pot.

5. The articles are then rinsed immediately under cold water.

6. The pot in which the articles were kashered is then itself kashered (see No. 4).

Open Flame: Any utensil which comes in direct contact with fire, such as a barbecue spit, a barbecue grill, a broiling pan or rack is kashered by open flame. The procedure is as follows:

1. The article to be kashered is thoroughly scoured.

2. The article is set aside and not used for 24 hours.

3. The article is then put under or over an open flame and thoroughly heated until the metal glows red hot or is so hot that a piece of paper is singed when it is touched to the metal.

Glassware: Glassware (including ovenproof ceramics) when washed is considered as new.[24]

Appliances

Ranges and ovens: The entire stove is thoroughly scoured. The burners or heating units are then turned on full until the metal glows red hot or a piece of paper is singed if touched to the metal. Be sure to remove all plastic knobs from around the oven to prevent them from melting.

Refrigerators/Freezers: The shelves and bins are removed in order to facilitate cleaning. The shelves, bins, and walls are then thoroughly washed.

Sink: A sink is kashered as a large pot, by scouring, filling with boiling water, and dropping a hot stone or hot piece of metal into it.

Dishwashers: The interior of the dishwasher is thoroughly scoured, paying careful attention to the strainer over the drain. The dishwasher is left unused for 24 hours and then run through a wash cycle without soap.

Small Appliances: Any metal surface of a small appliance that comes in contact with food should be kashered by purging. Plastic parts that can tolerate high heat should also be immersed. For example, an electric frying pan which can be immersed should be purged. Many electrical appliances cannot be immersed and therefore cannot be kashered. An electric mixer should have its beaters purged, and its bowls either purged (metal) or washed (glass). An electric can opener should have its blade and magnets removed and purged. The rest of the appliance should be cleaned so that no food is left in any crevices.

Countertops and Tables

Countertops and tables made of Formica or Arborite should be thoroughly scoured. Those made of wood are scraped with a steel brush. The surface is then left bare for 24 hours. After that the surface is completely splashed with boiling water, poured directly from the pot in which the water was boiled. For Passover, it is customary to cover all surfaces with paper, plastic, or other material.

Additives

Chemical additives to food products present difficult halakhic problems. Many additives are complicated compounds whose origin is difficult to ascertain. They may derive either from milk substances or from animal substances. In the former case, the question is whether they may be used together with meat. In the latter case, the problem involves the source of the animal substance— whether a clean or an unclean animal and whether the derivative can be used with milk products.

In approaching these questions it should be noted that, according to the laws of kashrut, not everything coming from an animal or a milk source necessarily retains the character of its source. The halakhic principles involved are:

1. *Pirsah b'almah*—mere secretion. This notion is applied by the rabbis (*Chullin* 116b) to secretions from the animal which have no food value. The classic example of this is rennet which is used in the curdling of cheese. Though this product may come from the organs of an animal, it ceases being considered an animal substance because it is not a real food but a secretion.

2. *Batel beshishim*. The rabbis developed the concept of *bittul*, annulment. This refers to the fact that even if the substance is in itself nonkosher, it is present in such minute amounts that it is assimilated totally into the permitted

element and is considered as if it did not exist. The amount usually required is a ratio of one (forbidden) to sixty (permitted).

3. *Davar chadash.* Sometimes the substance is so altered in the process of production that it bears little resemblance to the original. In this case, it does not share the characteristics of its original form. An example of this is gelatin which, though coming from an animal substance, is so altered in the course of production that it cannot be considered in the same category as animal substances. (See Klein, *1969 Proceedings of the Rabbinical Assembly*, pp. 203-218.)

The following is a list of commonly used additives. We have indicated whether products containing these chemicals can be used and/or if they can be used with milk and meat dishes.

Food scientists agree that the additives listed below have so changed in their nature that they no longer have the same physical/chemical make-up they originally had. **Unless otherwise indicated, the chemicals listed below are kosher and pareve.** We have indicated the original source of the product (s), its use in food products (u), and, if the information is available, the percentage commonly used (%).[25]

ADIPIC ACID—(s) beet juice; (u) baking powders, intermediate; (%) na

AGAR AGAR—(s) seaweed; (u) gelling; (%) 1-2%

ALUM/ALUMINUM SULFATE—(s) chemical; (u) in clarifying oils; (%) na

ARGOL—(s) grapes [see section on wine]; (u) in cream of tartar; (%) na

BHA—(s) synthetic; (u) anti-oxidant; (%) less than 1%

BHT—(s) synthetic; (u) anti-oxidant; (%) 200 parts/million

CALCIUM CARBONATE—(s) mineral; (u) deacidulant; (%) na

CALCIUM PROPIONATE—(s) synthetic; (u) preservative; (%) na

CALCIUM STEARATE—(s) animal or veg.; (u) binder or emulsifier; (%) na

CALCIUM STEAROL LACTYLATE—(s) soy; (u) conditioner; (%) 0.5%

CARAGHEEN—(s) red algae; (u) gelling, clarifying; (%) .025-.15%

CASEIN—(s) milk protein; (u) cheese; (%) na [dairy]

CITRIC ACID/POTASSIUM CITRATE/SODIUM CITRATE— (s) fruits; (u) acidulant; (%) na

CREAM OF TARTAR—(s) argol [grapes]; (u) baking; (%) na

DEXTROSE—(s) breakdown of starch; (u) sugar; (%) na

GELATIN—(s) animal; (u) gelling; (%) na [see Klein, "Is Gelatin Kosher?"]

GLUCOSE—(s) veg; (u) sugar; (%) na

GLYCERINE—(s) animal, veg. or petr.; (u) sweetener; (%) na

GLYCINE—(s) hydrolysis of gelatin; (u) binder, sweetener; (%) na

GUM ARABIC—(s) veg.; (u) thickener, emulsifier; (%) na

LACTIC ACID—(s) veg.°; (u) acidulant; (%) na

LACTOSE—(s) milk sugar; (u) sweetener; (%) na [dairy]

LAURIC FATS—(s) veg.; (u) cocoa butter sub.; (%) na

LECITHIN—(s) soy and corn oil; (u) emulsifier; (%) 1-2% of fat

MAGNESIUM STEARATE—(s) animal or veg.; (u) emulsifier; (%) na

MONO AND DI-GLYCERIDES—(s) animal or veg.; (u) emulsifier, etc.; (%) 0-5%. [A complete response on mono and di-glycerides is available from the Rabbinical Assembly Committee on Jewish Law and Standards.]

MONOSODIUM GLUTAMATE—(s) veg.; (u) flavor enhancer; (%) na

OLEIC ACID—(s) chemical; (u) na; (%) na

PECTIN—(s) fruit; (u) enzyme; (%) na

PEPSIN—(s) animal; (u) enzyme; (%) na

POLYSORBATE 60/80—(s) animal or veg.; (u) emulsifier, etc.; (%) .008-.5%

° Only lactic acid used in cream cheese is dairy.

PROPYLENE GLYCOL—(s) synthetic; (u) emulsifier, etc.; (%) 0-30% of ingredient

RENNET—(s) synthetic or animal [*see* cheese]; (u) curdling; (%) na

SODIUM ALGINATE—(s) seaweed; (u) stabilizer; (%) na

SODIUM BENZOATE—(s) synthetic; (u) preservative; (%) na

SODIUM CASEINATE—(s) cow's milk; (u) flavor, etc.; (%) 1-5% [dairy]

SODIUM PROPINATE—(s) synthetic; (u) preservative; (%) na

SODIUM LAURYL SULFATE—(s) synthetic; (u) whipping agent; (%) na

SORBIC ACID—(s) synthetic; (u) acidulant, anti-oxidant; (%) na

SORBITAN MONOSTEARATE—(s) animal or veg.; (u) emulsifier; (5) less than 2%

SORBITAL—(s) veg.; (u) sweetener; (%) na

SPAN/TWEEN—*see* polysorbate 80

STEARIC ACID—(s) animal or veg.; (u) fatty acids; (%) na

SULFUR DIOXIDE—(s) synthetic; (u) preservative; (%) na

VEGETABLE GUMS—(s) veg.; (u) gum; (%) na

VEGETABLE SHORTENINGS—The term vegetable shortening or 100% pure vegetable shortening on a product means that all of the fats used in the shortening are vegetable based. Manufacturers, however, can add emulsifiers of miscellaneous origins to the shortenings.

WHEY—(s) cow's milk; (u) flavor; (%) na [dairy]

NOTES TO
THE JEWISH DIETARY LAWS

Their Meaning for Our Time

[1] See Nathan Glazer's *American Judaism* (University of Chicago Press, 1957) and Will Herberg's *Protestant, Catholic, and Jew* (Doubleday, 1955).

[2] This does not mean that Judaism is simply a religion of *halakhah*, advocating only the keeping of the law as a kind of "sacred physics" (Abraham J. Heschel), without concern for principles. Indeed, the mechanical observance of the laws of Kashrut without any proper understanding of what one is about, of the meaning of what one is doing—as, unfortunately, is all too often the case—is a denial of the very purpose of the Torah. One can obey the Law meticulously, wrote Nachmanides, and yet be a hateful person. Likewise, he might well have added, one can obey all the regulations of Kashrut and yet be a glutton. Doing must lead to thinking and activity to attitude. Concern for the spirit is equally a part of Judaism.

[3] Chulin 84a

[4] P'sachim 49b

[5] B'reshit Rabah 33:3; Bava M'tzia 85a

[6] Moses had difficulty restraining the craving of the Hebrews for the "flesh pots" of Egypt. Nor did the heavenly manna satisfy their appetites. Thus Moses was forced to arrange a flesh meal for the evening (Yoma 75b). Again, the rabble among them "fell a-lusting" and demanded more meat (Num. 11:4). They were then supplied in good measure with quails from the sea, which, however, caused an epidemic (Num. 11:31-34; comp. Ps. 128:25-31).

[7] *Guide of the Perplexed*, Friedlander translation, Part III, Chapter 48, p. 253.

[8]The Hebrew word is *alehem*.

[9]This does not mean that "reasons" have not been given for the separation of milk and meat. The Targum already understood the verse "Thou shalt not cook a kid in its mother's milk," in this larger sense. According to Maimonides the Biblical prohibition had its origin in the fact that the pagan cults of Canaan practiced a fertility rite which was particularly abominable and which revolted the Jews: the cooking of a kid in its mother's milk. Another "reason" advanced by Dr. Abraham J. Heschel for the prohibition may be that the goat—for us more commonly the cow—generously and steadfastedly provides man with the single most perfect food he possesses: milk. It is the only food which, by reason of its proper composition of fat, carbohydrate and protein, can by itself sustain the human body. How ungrateful and callous we would be to take the child of an animal to whom we are so indebted and cook it in the very milk which nourishes us and is given us so freely by its mother.

A Guide to Observance

[1]Exodus 23:19, 34:26, and Deuteronomy 14:21.

[2]For an excellent discussion of the legal basis of the time separation between meat and milk, see Isidore Grunfeld, *The Jewish Dietary Laws*, Vol. 1, Soncino Press, London, 1972, pp. 123 ff.

[3]*She'elot u'Teshuvot Hakham Zevi*, #75 and *Medini, Sedeh Hemed*, under *Chametz Umatzah*, Vol. 7, p. 178.

[4]*Orach Chayim* 451:26.

[5]Archives of the Committee on Jewish Law and Standards of the Rabbinical Assembly, Letter from Eugene H. Fontana, Director of Physical Properties Research Department, Corning Glass Works, July 19, 1979.

[6]Klein, *Guide*, pp. 369-370 and Efrati, *Sha'arai Halakhah*, sec. 4, pp. 29-33. Shaul Ovadya in *Magen B'edi* maintains that meat and dairy dishes can be washed in the same machine without the rinse cycle (#19, pp. 102-111).

[7] For special Passover regulations, see the section on Passover.

[8] *Pareve* may be used with meat or dairy foods.

[9] The question of cheese is thoroughly explored in a responsum by the late Rabbi Isaac Klein, included in his book, *Responsa and Halakhic Studies*, pp. 43-58.

[10] For a full discussion of blood spots in eggs, see Grunfeld, *The Jewish Dietary Laws*, pp. 113-114.

[11] The deer is also a permitted animal; however, it would have to be ritually slaughtered in order for the meat to be kosher.

[12] Nondomestic geese, specifically swan geese, are not kosher.

[13] The Bible does not list general principles for distinguishing kosher from nonkosher fowl, but lists forbidden species. The rabbis of the Talmud derived specific characteristics which all permitted birds have in common.

[14] The anatomical details involved in *bedikah* are excellently described in Klein, *Guide*, pp. 314 ff.

[15] The term *glatt* means "smooth." It refers to the practice of using only those animals whose lungs are smooth, free of any *sirkhot* (adhesions). The insistence on "glatt kosher" is an additional stringency which was largely introduced into the U.S. by emigres from Eastern Europe after World War II. Since the codes of Jewish law indicate which lesions render the animal unfit, and how to determine this, the insistence that all meat be "glatt" seems to be an unnecessary burden on those who observe kashrut.

[16] Fowl or other meat should not be placed in boiling or hot water for cleaning purposes before it is kashered. Hot water causes the blood to coagulate, making it impossible to purge it by soaking and salting.

[17] Report of the Committee on Jewish Law and Standards of the Rabbinical Assembly of America, 1953 *Proceedings*, p. 40.

[18] The responsum by Rabbi Israel Silverman on this subject can be read in *Conservative Judaism and Jewish Law* (Seymour Siegel, ed.), pp. 308-316.

[19] A home test for the presence of starch in a pill or tablet is as follows: (1) Crush the pill or empty the capsule. (2) Add a drop of tincture of iodine. (3) If the mixture reacts by turning a deep blue-black, it contains starch. As in all cases, when a question arises, consult a rabbi. (Kashrus Division, Student Organization of Yeshiva Rabbi Isaac Elchanan Theological Seminary, *A Guide to Kashrus and Yom Tov*, New York, 1971, p. 105.)

[20] A guide to the kosher restaurants in the United States is found in *The Second Jewish Catalogue* by Michael and Sharon Strassfeld. Also, in the London Jewish Chronicle's *Jewish Travel Guide*.

[21] Information concerning Jewish activities on college campuses is available from Leader's Training Fellowship, 3080 Broadway, New York, NY 10027; B'nai B'rith Hillel Foundation, 1640 Rhode Island Avenue, Washington, DC 20036; National Council of Young Israel, 3 West 16th Street, New York, NY 10003.

[22] See Klein, *Guide*, pp. 87 ff.

[23] A full discussion of *challah* is found in Grunfeld, *Jewish Dietary Laws*, Vol. II, pp. 56 ff.

[24] In regard to glassware, the *Shulchan Arukh (Orach Chayim* 451:26) states: "Glass utensils do not require any '*hekhsher*' because they do not absorb." There are differing views, however. Rabbi Moses Isserles (*ad loc*): "Even purging (glass) is ineffective." Rabbi Abraham Danzig (*Chayei Adam* 124:22) writes that the proper method to kasher glassware is to soak it in clear water for 72 hours, changing the water every 24 hours.

[25] Much of this information is taken from the *Handbook of Food Additives*, edited by Thomas Furia and published by the Chemical Rubber Corporation, Akron, Ohio.

Selected Bibliography

Grunfeld, Isidore, *The Jewish Dietary Laws*, London: Soncino, 1972. The most complete book in English on the Dietary Laws.

Klein, Isaac, *Responsa and Halakhic Studies*, New York: Ktav, 1975.

_____. *A Guide to Jewish Religious Practice*, New York, Jewish Theological Seminary, 1979.

_____, "The Kashrut of Cheeses," *Conservative Judaism* 28:2 (Winter 1974), 34-36.

_____, "Swordfish," Proceedings of the Rabbinical Assembly 30 (1966), 111-115.

_____, "Is Gelatin Kosher?" *Proceedings of the Rabbinical Assembly*, 1969. Rabbi Klein did much of the pioneering work in Kashrut and other halakhic issues for the Conservative Movement.

Rubenstein, S.L., *The Book of Kashrut*, New York: Self-published, 1967.

Silverman, Israel, "Are All Wines Kosher?" in *Conservative Judaism and Jewish Law*, edited by Seymour Siegel, New York: Rabbinical Assembly, 307-316.

Union of Orthodox Jewish Congregations of America and Rabbinical Council of America, *Kashruth: Handbook for Home and School*, New York: Joint Kashruth Commission, 1972.

Yeshiva University Student Organization, Kashrus Division, *A Guide to Kashrus and Yom Tov*, New York: 1971.

_____, *A Guide to Kashrus*, 1974.

INDEX